THE GIRL WHOSE MOTHER ROBBED A BANK

Wendy Storer

Published in 2024 by Amazon

**The Girl Whose Mother Robbed a Bank
Copyright © 2024 Wendy Storer**

The author asserts their moral right under the Copyright Designs and Patents Act, 1988 to be identified as the author of this work.

All rights reserve. No part of this publication may be reproduced, copied, stored in a retrieval system or transmitted, in any form or by any means, without the prior written consent of the copyright holder, nor be otherwise circulated in any form of binding or cover other than that in which it is published and without a similar condition being imposed on the subsequent purchaser.

All characters in this work are fictional.
Any resemblance to real persons, either living or dead, is purely coincidental.

For Lauren, Dave and Heather

The Girl Whose Mother Robbed a Bank

1.

The robbery happened when I was eight. We were in the West Bank on Knott Street. Mum had one broken arm and one tattooed arm. She wanted a loan to get her tattoo inked over. It was a beautiful purple butterfly with 'I ♥ the Purple Emperor' written underneath in fancy writing.

The bank wouldn't give her the money.

She argued with them, but they still wouldn't give it to her. She shouted, and yelled and took off her jumper to show everyone the butterfly. She was wearing a black lace bra and didn't care who saw. Nobody looked at the butterfly. I wanted to be somewhere else. Not just because of the argument or my embarrassment, but because I didn't want to be there in the first place. I liked the butterfly. It was pretty and purple was my favourite colour.

And then suddenly a man in a plastic mask started shouting to get on the ground. I wasn't supposed to know it was Billy Slade, but it was and I did.

Everyone screamed.

There was a gunshot and Mum pushed me to the floor.

An alarm went off.

"Play dead," whispered Mum in my ear.

It was a game we use to play a lot, especially when she had a man friend over, so I knew exactly what to do. I closed my eyes tight and lay rock still. Didn't matter what was going on around me, I just had to stay like that until Mum gave me the all-clear.

I was good.

Very good.

Afterwards, when the policemen came, Mum wasn't there. Billy Slade and his gang went to prison. I went into foster care. They told me Mum was 'implicated' in the robbery, but it wasn't like that. We were there because of the butterfly and she was in the wrong place, at the wrong time.

>53 Ocean Avenue,
>Cockle Bay,
>MB11 2EQ

Me again. New address.

My last chance…

After this I'm looking at a hostel, or standing on street corners begging strangers for money, a big mac or a sleeping bag. Unless of course a miracle occurs and you come galloping in like some diva knight in shining armour on your faithful steed, arms outstretched, chocolates in hand and a rose between your teeth to rescue me, your one and only darling daughter...

Sometimes I close my eyes and imagine we're together – in OUR flat, eating OUR take-away, watching OUR telly, wearing face packs, pyjamas and fluffy slippers – or whatever it is mums and their daughters are supposed to do. And sometimes that movie in my head is so clear it's real. I smile inside and out and I want the feeling to last forever. But when I open my eyes it's gone. You're gone. The sunshine has gone. I'm just Elle again.

The family I'm with now are called 'the Loves'. Sid – the Dad – is an actor, most famous for being the feet in a foot deodorant advert. Mo – the mum – bakes cakes. Her Dad, Green, also lives here. He's old and crabby and so far we've barely said two words. He definitely doesn't like me. There's another care kid too, Olivia, she's 5… And did I mention they were my LAST CHANCE before a hostel? No pressure or anything.

I'll be seventeen in September, but rescue operations before that date would be greatly appreciated. Failing that, please write back. I won't tell anyone where you are.

Love you always,

Elle xxx

2.

Writing to Mum is taking a loan from the Bank of Hope. This time, I'll get a reply.

I take stamps and a tenner from Mo's purse, but when I look up Green is there, staring but vacant. Green (think Doc Brown in *Back to the Future*) skull-like and possessed, with crazy white hair. I shove the contraband up my sleeve and can't work out if he saw me or not. If he did, I've blown it already.

"I'm going out," I call to Mo, trying not to think about worst case scenarios.

Mo (think Melissa McCarthy, *Bridesmaids, Identity Thief, Ghostbusters*) appears in the hallway, wiping her sweaty forehead with a floury hand. "Out Luvvy? Why?"

"Erm, to get to know the area?" I say. Rookie mistake. The hesitation and the question mark make it sound like a lie.

So Mo says, "I'll come with you once the buns are done. Twenty minutes?"

"No! I'm good! Really. I like exploring, you know … and getting to know places." I try to sound committed to a course of action I have no intention of carrying out.

"But you might get lost." She's worried I'll do something reckless like get pissed, set fire to a waste bin, or rob a bank.

"I won't go far," I say, innocent smile, sweet pleading eyes.

Mo bumps the living room door open with her massive arse rather than get flour on the door handles. "What do you think, Sid?" she says.

Sid and Olivia are on the floor building a tower from toilet roll tubes.

"Sid!" she says, louder. "What do you think?"

"What? What's that?" Sid (think Jim Carrey, *Bruce Almighty, Lemony Snicket, Ace Ventura*) doesn't even look up.

"Do you think Elle is okay to explore? Alone?"

Meanwhile Olivia's Batman doll balances precariously on the edge of a cardboard tower. "Don't do it, Batman," says Sid, in his out-of-work-actor's phony American accent. Olivia (think, *Amanda Thripp in Matilda* ... or better still, think brat) makes Batman jump, smashing the tower. "KAPOW!" she shouts.

Toilet roll tubes fly everywhere.

Sid, phony accent, cries, "Batman's dead! Batman's dead! Our Superhero is dead!"

Olivia pulls Batman from the cardboard rubble and shouts, "No, Robin! I'm alive!" and flies Batman through the air turning somersaults while Sid sings the Batman theme tune.

I resist the temptation to tell them Batman can't fly.

"Sid!" says Mo, impatiently. "Elle wants to go out."

Sigh. It's not a crime. There doesn't have to be a fuss. "I won't go far," I say. "Promise. I just need some fresh air."

That's when Green limps in from the garden, stuffing his face from an open packet of Ginger Nuts. He doesn't offer one to anyone else and if I did the same I'd get a polite reminder to share. I don't mention this. I'm new here, after all.

Fingers crossed he doesn't mention the letter, stamps or tenner.

"I'm going for my paper," he says, spraying biscuit crumbs everywhere.

Mo's face bursts into a big smile. "That's perfect! Elle can walk with you."

This is horrific.

Green tucks the biscuits in his jacket pocket and looks me up and down.

Mo leans over and whispers, conspiratorially, "He needs someone to keep him out of mischief."

We all know it's really the other way round.

Mo goes back to her buns and it's just me and mad old Doc Brown off to the shops. He's about as overjoyed as I am, but resistance is futile. (That's a line from Star Trek, by the way. I'm not into Sci Fi, but even in real life it's relevant.)

The Love's house is different to others on Ocean Avenue. Instead of paved driveways and sculptured hedges, they've got sinkholes, a weed jungle and rusty old pram wheels leaning up against the wall. Their antique orange campervan blocks light into the living room and bird nests block the gutter. It was raining when I arrived and the front doorstep looked like Niagara Falls. It's not raining today, but there are still puddles to dodge.

On the street, Green stumbles. He is the slowest walker in the history of time and I feel my patience bubbling under the surface like volcano lava, about to explode, except that when a motorbike roars past breaking the sound barrier with its drum and bass engine racket it's Green who erupts.

His face turns red and he's apoplectic with rage, waving his stick, shouting. "You'll kill someone, you maniac!" And then he trips up, like, proper lurches and I have to catch him before he falls. "I got his number," he growls, pulling a pen from his inside pocket, face still red. "Write it down before I forget."

"Where?"

"On that letter up your sleeve."

My heart beat smashes the sound barrier. I grab my arm instinctively. The letters are between me and Mum and if anyone else ever gets wind it could be the end of a beautiful relationship. It could mean prison. Playing dumb is my only defence. "I don't know what you're talking about."

"Just write this down!" he barks.

Mo told me he used to be in the police and that – along with his mad red face – is kind of intimidating, so I do as I'm told and when I'm done Green snatches the envelope away.

"That's mine!" I protest. "Give it back."

I watch it disappear into his jacket pocket with the Ginger Nuts. He taps his nose and starts walking again, or rather, lurching and stumbling and stopping every few steps. I'm no pickpocket, but if he *were* to fall and I *didn't* save him – which doesn't look out of the realms of possibility – I just might be able to get the letter back.

We reach the Holy Grail – a post box – outside Max's Corner Shop. Miraculously, Green is still upright and now very alert. The bike which gave Green apoplexy is parked next to the post box.

"What do you think?" he says.

"What do you mean, *what do I think*?"

He points at the bike. "Of that."

It's black and chrome with high handle bars, a low seat, and a Harley badge on the engine. Billy Slade (think, Jack Black, *School of Rock*, only badass) used to ride a Harley.

"It's disgusting," I say. Not because of the way it looks; I don't care what it looks like. It's disgusting because of the memories it triggers. The bad ones. Put them together, sit yourself down with a box of popcorn, and you've got front row seats at the disaster movie of Elle Mackenzie's life; *The Girl Whose Mother Robbed a Bank*, now showing at a cinema near you.

Green laughs. "Good girl," he says, and hands me a 50p piece. "Get me a Gazette," he says. "And a comic for Olivia. Something with Batman or Spiderman on the front. I'll wait here."

I stare at the money.

"What are you waiting for?" he grumbles.

"More than this?" I say.

He doesn't argue; just digs in his pocket, pulls out the Ginger Nuts, my letter, and finally a crumpled five pound note. "Now do as you're told and buy me a paper," he growls.

I watch him stuff the letter back into his pocket, followed by the biscuits, wondering what he'll do when he reads it.

*

Inside the shop, the leather-clad biker – still wearing his helmet – is arguing with the girl on the till about a sign on the wall.

MOTORCYCLE HELMETS MUST BE REMOVED BEFORE ENTERING THE PREMISES.

"If you want this off," he's saying, knuckle-knocking his titanium headgear, "you should put the notice *OUTSIDE*, so I can read it *BEFORE* I come in."

He has a point.

The girl at the till is apologetic, but won't serve him until the helmet is removed.

He argues about the relevance of an entirely visible face and why a helmet makes any difference to a tobacco purchase, but she's wedded to the rules and refuses to budge. Their voices are rising. He's moved on from knuckle-knocking the helmet to fist thumping the counter. Again I am reminded of Billy Slade and I don't like it, so I grab a Gazette, pocket some fruit pastilles while no one is looking and loiter by the cake cabinet scanning for a quick exit in case it all kicks off. And then this man carrying a small dog wanders in, picks up a paper, waits behind Helmet Head at the counter, doesn't get served on account of Till Girl having her hands full and eventually joins in. He's on her side, obviously.

I don't want anything to do with arguments and bikers, but I can't just leave because they're in the way. And then this Miriam Margolyes look alike (think, Professor Sprout, *Harry Potter and the Chamber of Secrets*) emerges from the STAFF ONLY door, effing and jeffing about *bikers this* and *bikers that*. And before you know it, hell has broken loose in Cockle Bay...

The dog is on the floor, yapping and snarling at the biker.

The biker swears and tries to kick him away.

The man pushes him, shouting to leave the dog alone.

The biker falls into a shelf of cans, knocking them all over the floor.

And Miriam Margolyes beats him over the helmet with a French stick.

When Helmet Head scrambles to his feet, he grabs a bottle of ketchup and smashes it on the counter, holding the jagged neck as a weapon, shouting, "Back off! Back off!" The spilled sauce looks like blood.

Everyone backs off and he leaves.

The door slams.

BANG!

And suddenly, it's all over.

The calm after the storm.

Till Girl, the man and his dog, and Miriam Margolyes just stand there, kind of like they're in shock. Like they can't believe what just happened. Just like after the bank robbery. My heart is beating fast, but when I breathe again it slows down. I open the fruit pastilles and eat one.

Eventually, the man with the dog turns and asks if I am all right. I half smile and walk up to the till. Stroke the dog. He's white with black patches on his body and one black eye. Cute. His owner tells me he's called Pirate and says bikers should be locked up to learn respect. I just nod and agree; anything to get away quickly.

Miriam gets on the phone to call the police.

The girl at the till isn't much older than me and she's quiet. We're both shaking; a familiar feeling for me, but I'm guessing it's probably not for her. I ask if she's okay. She nods, but she's definitely not. I offer her Green's fiver for the paper.

"Keep it," she says.

*

Outside, Green is laughing.

Helmet Head is half way down the hill, pushing his bike. The tyres are flat.

"Did you see what just happened in there?" I'm still shaking.

Green looks at the shop. "No, what?" but he doesn't wait for an answer. He starts walking back towards Ocean Avenue, chuckling away to himself, no idea what I've just been through.

"There was a fight," I say. "The biker caused it but he kicked a dog and an old man pushed him over and now they're calling the police."

"Good," says Green, still walking, not interested. I thought he would have been, but he's too busy chuckling to himself.

We walk on, together, alone, not speaking.

I hear a siren in the distance and wonder if that's the police on their way to Max's Corner Shop and if I should go back and give a witness statement. It wouldn't be the first time.

And then Green stops abruptly in front of me, grabs the Gazette from my shaking hand and demands Olivia's comic.

"I forgot. It was awful in there."

"Then I want the change," he says, holding out his hand. Something falls from his sleeve.

I bend down to pick it up. It's a penknife. "Is this yours?"

"It might be," says Green, laughing, tucking the knife into his already overcrowded pocket. "What about my change?" he says, holding his hand out again.

I hand over the fiver.

He tucks that away too and doesn't ask why it's still a whole fiver or why the Gazette was apparently free. He doesn't seem to care I'm a trembling wreck. I've played a few impractical jokes in my time, but I'm young, in care, *troubled, wicked, lazy, dishonest...* etc (the definitive list of what it is to be Elle Mackenzie, on record at a Social Services near you) while Green is as old as history and supposed to be a responsible adult, so it doesn't add up. When he laughs ALL the way home, every fibre of my body screams, GREEN IS MAD.

3.

Sid's cooking today because Mo has book-keeping to catch up on. He's cooked rice with chicken, peas, onions and other alien ingredients I can't identify. He tells me it's called Siddy Kiddy's rice and it's his favourite because it's something his mum used to make. My mum only ever cooked a meal from scratch once. It was Halloween and she was showing off in front of Billy Slade. She made instant mash potato ghosts with frozen pea eyes and tinned spaghetti hair; otherwise, we lived on take-away, ready meals, and air.

Sid, Olivia, Green and I sit down at the table. The rice is in a serving dish in the middle of the table and Green helps himself. I don't take much because I'm not sure I'll like it. Sid serves a small amount onto a Peter Rabbit plate for Olivia and a larger amount onto a plain white dinner plate for Mo. He leaves hers on the side for later. I eat, nervous at first in case it's disgusting, but actually it's good enough to ask for seconds.

Olivia doesn't touch hers.

"What's the matter, Honey?" says Sid, encouraging her to pick up her fork.

"I'm on hunger strike," she says.

Sid laughs out loud. "Hunger strike? How do you know about hunger strikes?"

Olivia doesn't answer.

"Come on, Sweetheart, Superheroes have to eat," cajoles Sid.

She pushes her food away, folds her arms and blows a raspberry.

"You can't be Wonder Woman if you stop growing," he says.

"I don't want to be Wonder Woman," says Olivia, arms still folded. "I want Batman."

"When did you last have him?" says Sid.

"Yesterday."

"You were giving him a bath, weren't you? Have you looked in the bathroom?"

"Not there," says Olivia.

"How about your bedroom?"

"Not there."

"Could you have left him in the camper van when we were playing hide and seek?"

"I had him after that," says Olivia.

Sid asks Green, "Have you seen him, Maurice?" Yeah, Maurice is his real name. Mo told me Olivia starting calling him Green because he spends so much time in the greenhouse and the name stuck.

"Are you accusing me?" Green spits when he speaks. Gross.

"No, of course not," says Sid.

Green curls a lip and shovels another forkful of rice into his mouth.

Sid turns to me. "Elle? Have you seen Batman by any chance?"

"Sorry," I smirk. "I don't really take much notice of *toys*."

"HE'S NOT A TOY!" screams Olivia.

She's right there. He's not a toy; he's a weapon. Olivia has used Batman to hit me at least three times already.

"We'll find him," reassures Sid. "Now just eat your rice and we'll look when lunch is over."

But Olivia picks up her plate and lobs it across the kitchen. It hits the wall. The plate breaks. Peter Rabbit is in pieces. Rice, chicken and alien veg dribble down to the floor.

And I laugh. I know I shouldn't but I can't help it.

Mo comes running in. "What's happening?"

Olivia sits back, arms folded again, nostrils flaring, chin stuck defiantly out, a 5 year-old horror story who'd make Hit-Girl look like a pussy cat. "BATMAN'S MISSING!" she shouts.

Mo looks at the food splattered wall. "I'm sure you didn't need to do that," she says, calm as anything. "We'll find Batman later."

"I want him now!" demands Olivia.

"You're eating lunch now," says Mo, firmly.

"No, I'm not!" says Little Miss Kick-Ass.

"Yes, you are," says Mo.

Sid picks up the debris. Green holds his head like it hurts, then pushes his plate of food away, stands and shuffles out of the room.

Olivia starts bawling. A part of me wants her to stop, because I just want to eat my meal in peace. Another part of me wants her to carry on, testing Mo and Sid's patience till they lose it and she gets sent to her room, or shouted at, or threatened with a move... *Sorry, Olivia, but this isn't working out. You have to go and live with another family* ... Schadenfreude, they call it; delighting in another's misfortune.

But a much smaller part of me feels sorry for Olivia because she can't help herself. Been there, done that, and lived to regret it...

Mo crouches down and holds Olivia's hand. "I know you're upset, Luvvy. Of course you're upset. But I promise we'll find Batman after lunch. He can't be far. And Batman would want you to eat, wouldn't he? Because Batman knows you need your strength."

Sid serves Olivia a new plate of rice, which looks like a risky strategy, but unbelievably she picks up a fork.

"That's my girl," says Sid.

She smiles, sweetly, Little Miss Perfect all of a sudden, as if there never was a problem, and she eats.

Yes, she actually eats.

And I can't help thinking this will only get worse before it gets better because what's Olivia learned from this? That broken Peter Rabbit plates and rice splattered walls are a perfectly acceptable bargaining tool? Tantrums are okay? She who shouts loudest, wins? It never did me any good ... otherwise I wouldn't have ended up here, in a house smelling of gingerbread with the threat of hostel living and eventual homelessness hanging over my head. Because yes, I've seen the stats and I know that at least a quarter of young people become homeless within three years of leaving foster care, hostel or no hostel. The way my luck runs, I'll be joining them.

Mo asks us to clear the plates.

Olivia takes hers to the sink and comes back for Sid and Green's plates. Along with the serving dishes, I clear my own plate and the salt and pepper.

"Thanks, girls," says Sid. "That's really helpful and we appreciate it."

"Yes, thank you both. Good work," says Mo, giving us the thumbs up.

So ... it's nice to be appreciated, but really? All we did was clear a plate or two. And Little Miss Bad Arse gets off scot free? She deserved to lose Batman. That's all I'm saying.

4.

Films are good. They take you out of yourself and help you imagine what it's like to live someone else's life instead of your own pitiful existence. Watching movies is what I do best, but Sid already told me he forgot to renew Netflix and they've never had Disney or Prime, so it's a DVD or nothing. I go over to the bookcase full of antique films and start looking for something to watch.

Of course, as soon as I mention watching a film, Olivia *needs* to watch a film too. Nobody *needs* to watch a film and somebody *needs* to mention that, but ho-hum not today. And now we have to watch something which is *suitable* for Olivia.

Yawn.

I pull out Aladdin, because everyone likes Aladdin, right? But no, not Olivia. It's got fireworks in it. She doesn't like fireworks.

Lion King? Nope, Scar's too mean.

Toy Story? Fireworks again.

Cinderella, Little Mermaid, Snow White? Too girly.

We end up with *Despicable Me*, which is one I've never seen. It's about this villain called Gru who uses three orphan girls – Margo, Edith and Agnes – to help him steal from his evil rival. Olivia loves it. I don't like the way he uses the girls, but long story short, Gru has a heart after all and ends up adopting them.

"Why are you crying?" says Olivia, when it's over.

Before I think of an answer, Mo pops her head around the door and announces, "Cake time!"

Olivia forgets the question and goes bonkers, jumping on furniture and screaming, "Cake! Cake! Cake!"

Sid passes me a tissue, but doesn't expect an answer to Olivia's question which is just as well because I don't have one. Why would anyone cry over a stupid film?

In the kitchen there is a fancy cake covered in yellow butter icing and chocolate flake sprinkles waiting on the table. It never made it to Max's because the icing was too sticky, which is their loss and our gain. It looks amazing. Olivia is as excited as I have ever seen her and for once I get where she is coming from.

Mo cuts us each a slice, but before I am allowed to eat mine I have to take some out to Green.

An uneven brick path separates the greenhouse from the kitchen. Stacked on the path are several bags of potting compost, a coiled hosepipe, two metal buckets, a broom, a large number of traffic cones and some broken garden furniture. Inside the greenhouse, Green is wearing a plastic apron and rubber gloves, rearranging cactuses. There's a magazine open on the floor with pictures of butterflies.

I knock on the glass door and slide it open. A foul smell wafts over and makes me gag. I wonder if Green's farted. "I've brought you some cake," I heave.

"Don't want it," he says, not even bothering to look at me.

"But ... but Mo said you'd like it. I'll leave it on the side."

"I don't want it," he says. "Go away."

"I don't want it, *THANK YOU,*" I say slowly and deliberately, making a point about manners while also taking the opportunity to cast my eyes over the mess, hoping I might see my letter.

And then he says, "Are you still here? I thought I told you to get lost. This is *my* greenhouse and it's private. P. R. I. A. V. T. What part of that do you not understand?" He pulls the door closed and turns back to his prickly plants.

He's no Gru, that's for sure.

Hours later, I'm still fuming about the way he talked to me. When Mo takes Olivia off to bed, Sid wonders if I'm all right.

"Why wouldn't I be?" I snap.

"You seem quiet, Honey, that's all. I just wondered how you're settling in."

I shrug. I don't know how to share my feelings about Green – that he's my evil nemesis, sent by God, the universe or social services to cause chaos and suffering, to punish me for all my fuck-ups. It's best to say nothing.

"You can always talk to Mo or me," says Sid. "If there's *anything* you don't like, *anything* we're doing wrong ... or *anything* you'd like done differently."

I wouldn't know where – or how – to start, so I shrug and turn back to the TV remote, surfing the channels for something half decent to watch.

"Because it must be hard, coming to a new family. Strange. I get that, but we just want whatever's best for you," he says. "And we're here for you, Elle. We want you to know that."

"Sure, thanks," I say again, hoping my body language will signal the end of the conversation.

"So ... are you? Okay?" he says, refusing to drop it.

"Can I just watch a film?" I say.

At last, Sid nods. "Of course. What do you want to watch?"

I wander over to the vintage DVD collection and pull out a few which have okay covers. I hold up one called *Groundhog Day*. "What's this about?"

"It's about a weatherman who is doomed to live the same day over and over again until he gets it right," says Sid. "I think you'll like it." He puts it in the DVD player without waiting for me to consider other options, so I guess we're watching *Groundhog Day*.

I'm confused at first. I don't understand what's happening, but I do get into the swing of it. This weather guy – Phil – is really unimpressed when he gets sent to some backwater for work and he just wants to go home. But he can't leave because he's snowed in and when he wakes up the next day, it's not actually the next day, but the same day starting over again because he's stuck in a time loop. So at first he messes around with it and does stupid things, and then – because every day he wakes up is the same day and nothing changes – he gets angry and frustrated and even tries to kill himself. But then he falls in love with this woman, Rita, and starts doing stuff to impress her. He learns French, learns the piano, does good deeds, learns how to sculpt ice, and it's all for show; he doesn't really care about this stuff at first, but the more good stuff he does the more he enjoys it and that's when things start to work out for him. He gets loads of chances to get it right, still living the same day over and over again, because he can remember everything he's learned on previous days ... but no one else can. He starts to help people, is kinder and even starts to enjoy his job. Eventually it's a new day and Phil says to Rita, *'Do you know what today is?'* And she says, *'No, what?'* And Phil says, *'Today is tomorrow. It happened. You're here...'* It's schmaltzy but kind of nice.

Sid tells me Groundhog Day is a metaphor for situations that repeat themselves. I laugh and tell him that's the story of my life, so he wonders if there's one day I would like to live over and over again and what I'd change if I had the chance. I think about the day of the robbery, but there's nothing I could have done to change anything. Although, maybe if I'd never told the police about the robbery in the first place things would be different now? And as soon as I set off thinking about that, my heart starts racing, I feel sick and get the urge to curl up in a ball and hide...

"Well?" ask Sid, waiting for an answer, smiling.

I smile back, trying to forget, trying to think of some other day I'd be willing to live over and over. I remember Stacey Nolan's shoes I filled with jam in the changing rooms and how no one else found it funny. I remember all the staffroom door handles I oiled and the how all the teachers moaned and swore. I remember the fire alarms I set off to give me a break from boring teachers; the tickings-off, the warnings about my behaviour, the detentions. Was any of it worth it? Probably not. But my back-fired pranks do still make me laugh.

"What's funny?" says Sid.

He's read my file; he probably knows about all this anyway so I settle for, "The day of the school nativity, when I was five."

"And why would you relive that day?" he wonders.

"Because when I tripped Mary up in the dress rehearsal, it cost me my acting debut! And I really wanted to be the star of the show."

Sid laughs. "Why? How?"

I shrug, and laugh too. "Why did I trip Mary? Because she was sooo smug," I say. "I was supposed to be Mary. I'd actually been chosen to be Mary. I was the *real* Mary. I'd done all the other rehearsals, I knew all the lines and I could even hold the baby the right way up. Plus, I could sing Away in a Manger all the way through. But I didn't have the right costume. All I had was an old blue dressing gown Mum found in a charity shop. Some of the other kids were a bit disgusted by the food stains down the front and some more mysterious stains round the back, but I didn't care. I was Mary. And Mary – the mother of Jesus – certainly wouldn't care, would she?"

"Absolutely not!" says Sid, trying not to laugh.

"Then, on the day of the show," I continue, "Cynthia Alexander brought in a brand new royal blue bed sheet – not a stain in sight – and the other kids were all, '*ooh let's use that instead*' and even I had to agree it was better than my dressing gown ... except that Cynthia's mum said only Cynthia was allowed to wear it!"

Sid gasps. "That's not fair!"

"Long story short; they said I could be a sheep instead! A sheep! I was mad. I didn't want to be a sheep. I wanted to be Mary. So I tripped Cynthia up in the dress rehearsal and she fell over and banged her head on a wooden block. As a punishment I had to sit in the classroom while they went ahead and did the play without me. All the mums and dads were there – even my mum – and then afterwards, she had a go at me in front of all the other mums and dads for dragging her there for nothing. It was awful."

"Wow!" says Sid, eyes wide. "That definitely sounds like something worth changing."

I nod. "I was traumatised for weeks."

"So, Groundhog Day scenario, what would you do differently?"

I think about the options. "I could hide the sheet? ... Or trip Mary up more discreetly so no one knew it was me? ... Or frame someone else for it?"

"Or just be a sheep?" suggests Sid.

And I say, "No way! I wanted to be Mary. I wanted to be an actor, a star; not some stupid sheep."

Sid sits back and stares at me, thoughtfully. "You want to be an actor?"

"Of course not," I say, my blush giving away the lie.

"But you wanted to be an actor then?" He's starting to annoy me.

I shrug. "Who wouldn't?"

Sid raises an eyebrow.

"What?"

"It's okay to have a dream. If you don't have a dream, you can't make a dream come true."

"Isn't that a song?" I say. I think I saw it in some godawful film.

He laughs. "Yes, it's a song, from South Pacific – before your time – but that doesn't mean it's not true. And sometimes dreams turn into reality."

"So do nightmares."

Sid nods and kind of looks at me, like he's weighing something up and then he says, "If you want to be an actor, you *can* say it out loud."

I shake my head. "Who'd have me, anyway?"

"What do you mean, *who'd have you*?"

"Well it's not like Steven Spielberg's knocking on the door, is it?"

"You never know what opportunities are around the corner," he says.

"Oh no, wait!" I say. "Because who's that out the window? Is that Peter Jackson and George Lucas? Have they just joined a massive queue of opportunities? I see them now: film crews, directors, BAFTA. Oh and look, there's Peter and George fighting their way to the front of the queue. If we're not careful Heat and Hello magazines will turn up in a minute begging for an exclusive and that would never do. I'm a ward of court and not supposed to be getting all this publicity."

Sid laughs. "You're funny," he says

I pull a stupid face, trying to be unfunny.

But he just laughs again. "Like it or not, you should be on the stage," he says.

"So tell me," I say, changing the subject. "What day would *you* live again?"

Sid thinks long and hard. And then, eventually, says, "The day my mum moved back to Cape Town. I'd throw her a party and tell her how much I love her, instead of refusing to drive her to the airport and sulking like a baby at home."

And I just don't know what to say to that.

5.

There are three wire trays of fresh bakes cooling on the side – cup cakes, lemon tarts and Chelsea buns. The kitchen smells sweet and yeasty, like a bakery, and I feel as if I'm in cake heaven. It's not a bad way to start the day.

And then Sasha arrives.

Sasha is my social worker. When she smiles she has incredible dimples and when we first met she reminded me of Miss Honey (the kind caring teacher in *Matilda*.) I know better now. She's more Ursula (manipulative, power crazy *Little Mermaid* sea witch) than Miss Honey, and she usually only turns up when she has some dastardly plan to cause general misery. My heart sinks. I didn't know she was coming today.

She's over-the-top apologetic; she didn't *mean* to be so early, didn't *mean* to spoil our breakfast, doesn't want to *get in the way*; why don't we just *ignore* her and take our time? ... and so on. But I can't ignore her. After all, she's here to control my life.

Mo offers her a seat, coffee, a cake ... and doesn't wait for answers; just fills the kettle, puts instant coffee in a mug and chooses Sasha a particularly large Chelsea bun which she refuses, patting her stomach, mumbling something about *her weight*.

"You've just missed Olivia and Sid," says Mo.

"They're not why I'm here," says Sasha, pulling something from her briefcase. She passes it to me. "Weston College," she says. "That's where we're going today."

Are we? I had no idea. I glance at Mo who looks as surprised as I feel.

"Take a look at the prospectus" says Ursula – sorry, Sasha. "See what you think."

She sits down. Mo hands her the mug of coffee. They chat about the weather, holidays and Mo's baking commitments, while I leaf through the pages of the prospectus pretending to be interested. When I've pretended long enough, I put the prospectus down and Sasha turns back to me.

"So Elle, Weston College. Today's visit is a formality, just to get a feel for the place. I've assured them you're keen to turn over a new leaf, put some effort into whatever course you choose and stop playing these silly pranks." She wags her finger when she mentions *the pranks*. Her nails are shimmering pink and beautifully manicured, unlike my own chewed stubs. "They'll treat you like an adult, but you have to behave like one. Understand?"

Of course I understand; although technically and legally an adult is eighteen.

"I think you'll like it," she adds. "It's not like school."

I haven't always hated school. Before Mum went missing, school was mostly okay – apart from the nativity incident. I liked writing stories, learned about Henry VIII and his six wives, and pyramids, and I liked singing. I had a best friend, Emily. We thought it was funny that Elle and Em were next to each other in the alphabet and we always sat next to each other in class. But I've been to six different schools since the robbery and at each new one I had every intention of making it work. But then the questions started: *Where do you come from? Where do you live? What are you doing here? What's it like in care?* Followed by the *poor you* pity and finally the truth, which always set me apart. In one school there were quite a few of us in care and we even had a designated teacher for 'looked-after' children, except the other foster kids all had contact time with their parents and I never did. Nobody could believe my mum had abandoned me. I punched a girl for saying Mum didn't love me and after that I was more *talked about*, than *talked to* ... and when you do stand up for yourself, they move you. 'Time to start over again, Elle,' they'd say. *Groundhog Day*.

Sasha insists Weston College will be different.

I can re-sit GCSEs if I want, but they do other courses too: hairdressing, health and social care, performing arts, car maintenance, sports, construction, catering, photography, film making and all sorts of other subjects. The only thing in its favour is that for once I won't be the only newbie, which means I won't be the only one answering questions.

*

We're met at the college by Mrs Someone-or-Other, one of the General Studies teachers. She's more Miss Trunchbull than Miss Honey to look at, except she smiles the whole time and can't stop going on about the *wonderful this* and the *award winning that*. She shows us around with two other girls, Zayna and Tess (and their mums) who also hope to be starting in September.

Our guided tour includes the science labs, food tech rooms, a purpose built restaurant for catering students, art studios, gym, sports fields, library, computer suite, classrooms, engineering centre, hairdressing salons, conference and seminar suites, performing arts suite with theatre, a fully equipped recording studio, darkroom... and more. Zayna asks lots of question about the different courses, but Tess is really only interested in the catering department. She wants to be a chef.

Zayna and Tess already know each other and Zayna asks where I went to school. I tell her I've just moved into the area. There are no other awkward questions and – apart from apparently having two mums with me – I think I get away with looking normal.

It's nothing like school and Sasha might possibly be right.

*

Back at The Love's, Sasha wants to see my bedroom before she leaves, presumably to check I'm not living in a windowless attic full of spiders, trolls and zombies. Mo suggests I give my room a quick tidy first, while they catch up on paperwork.

My room is small and yellow, with a wooden framed bed, shelves and a wardrobe. There are pictures of kittens and puppies on the wall. I'm not especially into kittens or puppies, but I appreciate the attempt to make it feel less like a punishment cell and more like somewhere a sixteen year-old might choose to be. Also, Mo threw away the heavy duty black bin bag when I arrived – used to carry of all my worldly possessions – and bought me a proper suitcase. It's turquoise with a zip lid, a front pocket, wheels and everything. I appreciate this too. She says I can keep it forever. Apart from the suitcase, my clothes and a phone given to me by Eileen and Geoff the previous carers but one, I don't own anything and tidying is just a case of picking dirty clothes off the floor and dumping them in the laundry basket on the landing.

"Can I come in?" says Sasha, later.

She looks around and I'm suddenly conscious of all the things I could have done to make the room tidier. The bed has not been made, there are cake crumbs everywhere and a puddle of cocoa I spilled on the carpet earlier.

Sasha pulls up the duvet and we sit on my bed. "So, tell me Elle, how's it going? Are you settling in?" She takes a fat wad of tissues from her handbag and drops them on the cocoa to soak it up. "Well?"

I tell her everything is okay, but I'm really only interested in one thing. "Do you know where my mum is?" I say.

"I would tell you if I knew." She looks genuinely sorry. "Stevie's still missing, but I promise if and when I hear *anything* I'll call you." Her foot presses the tissues into the cocoa.

I look at her face for hints of a lie. I can't see any, but I'm desperate for a lifeline. "And when she does comes back," I say. "Can I live with her again?"

Sasha pulls a face and takes time to choose her words. "You're in our care now, which means legally your mother can't just walk in and take you back."

"Why not?"

Sasha takes a deep breath in, and then breathes out shaking her head. "Your mother is still wanted in connection with a bank robbery and her innocence would need proving before we embark on any parental fitness assessment."

I want to defend Mum, but obviously I can't.

We sit in silence for a while; me thinking about Mum, and Sasha looking around at the kittens and puppies and the mess I neglected to tidy away. I hear

35

Olivia and Sid in the garden, chasing each other around the tree, playing superheroes, and laughing. They get on like a house on fire. I wonder why Olivia is in care and where *her* real mum and dad are.

"What about Mo and Sid?" says Sasha, breaking me free from my thoughts.

"What about them?"

"Are you finding them easy to get on with?"

"They're nice." Not a lie.

Sasha picks up the cocoa laden tissues and drops them into the bin. "And Maurice? How are you finding him?" I'm scared she knows about the letter.

"Erm, he's nice too," I say. Definitely a lie.

Sasha laughs. "He's not the easiest person in the world to live with, but his heart is in the right place."

I bite my tongue. I doubt Green has a heart. He's a half-mad miserable old copper who's probably locked up dozens of criminals and maybe some innocents too. I wonder how he can live with himself.

"And finally, Olivia?" Sasha wonders. "How are things with Olivia?"

"What do you mean?"

"I mean, do you get on?"

"She's a laugh a minute," I say, dryly.

"Oh that's wonderful to hear," says Sasha, her sarcasm radar clearly faulty. "I remember reading something in your file from years back about wanting a little sister…"

Really? Because I definitely don't want one now.

"…So this is all very encouraging..." blah blah blah. On and on and on about Mo and Sid and Olivia and Weston College and prospects and all sorts of stuff but I'm not really paying attention anymore and I just wish she'd leave. But then she notices my suitcase. "... And this must be the new suitcase?" she says, pulling Mo's turquoise gift towards her, unzipping the lid...

And at EXACTLY that moment, I remember what is inside.

Sasha's eyes fall on Olivia's headless Batman.

I slam the lid back down, knowing resistance is futile.

"Elle? What's this?" Stupid question. She knows exactly what it is.

I open my mouth to lie except I can't find the words.

"Isn't this Olivia's Batman?" she says. "Isn't it the one she lost the other day? Mo tells me she was very upset."

I still don't have an answer.

And then Sasha looks me in the eye, waiting on a logical explanation for the dead *superhero* who isn't technically a superhero, especially not now.

I chew the inside of my cheek.

"Did you hide it because you broke it? Or did you take it and then break it?" she says.

"Neither?" I say. I consider telling her about how Olivia had used it as a weapon against me, but that would only get her into trouble as well and I'm not a grass.

"So how did it get in here?"

"I don't know?"

I try to look innocent, but my eyes dart instantly to the ten pound note on my chest of drawers, next to the ring I stole from Mo's bedroom. Sasha doesn't miss a thing.

"Elle! You cannot steal from your foster carers. We've been through this ... how many times? Stealing is wrong."

"I didn't steal anything!" I say.

"So what's Batman doing here? And this ring? And where did you get this money?"

"I don't know! Honest. Maybe someone planted them to make me look guilty?" I can't help but smile.

Sasha raises an eyebrow and tips her head. "It's not funny," she says. "Mo and Sid have made a commitment to look after you and to trust you as an equal and *honest* family member..."

I chew my lip.

"...Because this is your *last chance*. I've done my very best to keep you with a family, because it's what you need and what you deserve. I know life has been tough for you, but if you can't behave and be honest and respect the people who have welcomed you into their lives, I won't be able to help you."

She blathers on about crimes and punishments, but I'm not listening. I'm cursing myself for not hiding Batman somewhere else, while mentally composing another letter to Mum.

"Or maybe it's for the best?" says Sasha. "What do you think?"

"Sorry? What do I think about what?"

She sighs. "Were you even listening to me?"

"Bits of it," I shrug.

She shakes her head, exasperated. "Then maybe a hostel *is* the best place for you."

"No!" I cry. "Please don't send me there. People who live in hostels are all weirdoes and psychopaths.

They nick your stuff to fund their drug habits and beat you up when you're asleep…"

"Stop it!" says Sasha. "You're scaring yourself. And it's not true." She looks at me and shakes her head. "But it won't be as nice as living here." She picks up the money, the ring and the pieces of Batman and tells me she'll meet me downstairs when I've had a chance to think about the *consequences* of my actions.

53 Ocean Avenue,
Cockle Bay,
MB11 2EQ.

Me again.

I have another new address. I might not be here that long. I've already written to you once, but Green – who just happens to be a mad old ex-copper – has it. I swear I didn't know he was watching me, but he was, and then he took it off me and now he's keeping it.

So this is kind of a warning. If you do get this letter you have to get out – QUICKLY – in case he's told anyone.

Also, please come back and rescue me.

I miss you so so much,

Elle x

6.

Mr Max usually collects Mo's baking before I'm out of bed, but he's short of staff today and Mo will need to deliver. On the outside, the camper van looks like a death trap. There's rust, peeling paint, and taped cardboard instead of a back window. Thankfully it's cleaner inside; there's a sink and cupboards and a seat where we put the trays. I don't think anyone will catch cholera, covid or the dreaded spotted lurgy from eating Mo's cakes.

I've got Mum's letter in my pocket.

At Max's we take the cake trays inside. Mo and Miriam Margolyes chat about the weather, about business being slow and a vomiting bug going around. Miriam tells Mo about the biker incident. She's surprised no one mentioned it and immediately checks I'm okay and apologises, but it wasn't her fault. I try to slip out to the post box, but Miriam calls me back and gives me two chocolate rabbits for being helpful – one wrapped in pink foil and one in blue. I remember to say thank you, but…

a) I'm not five years old,

b) I can't post mum's letter, and

c) Even though Mo compliments my kindness and helpfulness and says she couldn't have done it all in one journey without me, when we get home I have to give Olivia one of the rabbits. She didn't even earn it!

"You don't need two," says Mo.

Olivia looks dead smug and takes the blue rabbit.

"But DON'T eat them until after lunch. Can't have you spoiling your appetites," says Mo.

We take the rabbits to our rooms and then Olivia – who seems to think the rabbits were my idea – gets all soppy and asks me to play dressing up. I tell her to get lost because I have more important things to do, like poke red hot needles in my eyes and rip out my fingers nails with iron pliers, but five minutes later she's standing in front of me with chocolate around her mouth.

"You weren't supposed to eat that until after lunch," I say.

"Eat what?" she says.

"Doh! Your chocolate rabbit," I say. "Mo will lose her shit!" She probably won't.

"I didn't eat it."

"There's chocolate around your mouth, idiot." But she's resolute. Shakes her head. "Didn't eat it."

"Did."

"Didn't."

"Did."

"Didn't," she says. "And I can prove it."

"Oh yeah?" I say. "How?"

She thumps up the stairs and back down again, smiling as if butter wouldn't melt in her mouth, and produces the BLUE rabbit!

What the fuck?!

I run to my own room and yes, my pink rabbit has gone. Olivia – SPAWN OF SATAN – has eaten it. And it's not even that I wanted it that much; it's the principal.

I run back downstairs screaming, "OLIVIA! I'm going to kill you!"

Sid grabs my arm. "I don't think so," he says.

"But she's eaten my rabbit!" I say, shaking myself free.

Olivia crawls out from behind the sofa, guilt plastered all round her mouth,

"You ate my rabbit," I spit. "And you're going to pay."

We stare at each other.

And Sid says, "What are you talking about?"

So I tell him about the rabbit rewards *I* earned for helping Mo at Max's. He looks at Olivia, and says, "Did you eat Elle's rabbit? Tell me the truth."

The monster child from hell replies, "Yes. Sorry," and smiles at me, all cocky and brash, because she knows there'll be no consequences.

"Good girl for telling the truth," says Sid.

GOOD GIRL FOR TELLING THE TRUTH???

"She can't just eat my rabbit and get away with it?" I say.

"No, of course not." says Sid. "But perhaps you could have hers? Olivia? Is that a good idea?"

"Okay!" she says, and hands the blue rabbit to me.

As soon as Sid is out of earshot, Olivia says, "I've licked it. I've licked it and rubbed bogeys on it too..." then skips off, laughing.

I stare at the foil wrapping which has definitely been dislodged. She won't get away with it. This is not the end.

*

I'm stuck inside with Melissa McCarthy and Doc Brown getting his knickers twisted about some dual carriageway they're planning for the bay. Sid and Little Miss Sticky-Fingers are in the garden making a Batmobile out of junk. They offered me the chance to join in, but I'm 16, still angry about the bunny incident and wishing I could be in town, wishing I had friends, wishing I could be having my own fun; except 'fun' usually ends up with me in a police car, a police station, or permanent exile in the Outer Hebrides.

"Are you all right, Elle?" wonders Mo. "You seem quiet."

I shrug.

"You can always talk to Sid or me if there's anything on your mind."

"Thank you," I say, thinking, *here we go again*. "Can I watch a film?" I say, stopping the speech before it starts.

And Mo says, "Yes, luvvy, of course you can."

And then, while I'm choosing one, she says, "Sid mentioned you wanted to be an actor."

"Erm... no," I say, pulling a where-did-he-get-that-ridiculous-idea-from face.

"It's just that there's an amateur dramatics group who meet at the town hall and..."

I grab *17 Again* because Zac Efron's in it.

"...and they're always looking for new blood."

I slide Zac straight into the DVD player. It clicks and whirs and I wait for the picture.

"... And I wondered if you fancied it. I'll come with you if you like," says Mo. "It might be fun."

I fast forward through the previews and credits. Mo carries on talking, but I've already hit play and I'm not even in the room now. I'm Scarlet, breaking the news to Mike (Zac). I'm pregnant and I'm scared, wondering what's going to happen to us. And because he's got this really important basketball game, I walk away ... it's not a good time ... but as I do, Zac comes running up behind me and takes me in his arms. We kiss. He tells me everything will be all right...

"When you're young, everything feels like the end of the world," says Mo.

It jolts me. I'm back in the room. "What?"

"It's a line from the film."

"I know." I've seen it a hundred times already.

"When you're young, everything feels like the end of the world," she says again. "But it's not. It's just the beginning."

I press pause and look at Mo, not sure whether to feel irritated or impressed.

She's smiling. "I love this film. Reminds me everything can change."

So I nod because it's true, everything can change, although rarely for the better.

But then she says, "So how about it? Fancy joining a drama group with me?"

I consider the idea briefly, but Zac is calling. "Thanks," I say. "But I'll pass."

And Mo says, "Okay, it was just an idea."

*

When the coast is clear for revenge I creep upstairs, crush the pre-licked blue chocolate bunny and put the pieces in a mug with a few drops of hot water from the bathroom tap. I sneak into Olivia's room, pull her duvet down and sprinkle the melting bunny parts onto her sheet, pull her duvet up and wriggle about on top. If I've done it right, there should be brown stains all over her sheets.

As I'm leaving her bedroom, I bump into Green on the landing. He narrows his eyes and looks me up and down as if to say *'what are you up to?'*, but I'm saved by the bell – the house phone – and fly down stairs to answer it and avoid awkward questions.

"Hello, who's speaking, please?" I say. Polite voice.

A woman tells me she is Melissa Martin, Sid's agent.

"One moment, please. I'll go and get him."

Green's still staring from up the stairs. He watches, but doesn't say a word and I go outside to get Sid.

"Melissa?" he says, excitedly. "Really?"

It's no big deal, but he acts like I've just announced Christmas is early. Drops everything. Hugs me. Thanks me. Tells me I'm wonderful. Tells Olivia not to touch a thing, and practically skips inside.

Weirdo.

I look at the Batmobile they're building. It's coming together nicely. Sid's clever with his hands and Olivia is lucky to have him indulging her superhero fantasies. He's joined some old planks of wood together, added a cardboard box seat, and attached some old pram wheels. I watch Olivia picking flowers and laying them across the front of the Batmobile to make it look pretty. I wonder if anyone has told her about headless Batman. I try to imagine how she'll react when she finds the bunny in her bed and wonder if I've gone too far, but then she picks up a hammer and starts waving it around.

"Sid told you not to touch anything," I say. "Put it down."

She laughs, doesn't put the hammer down and instead picks up a nail and starts hammering it into a tree, watching my reaction.

"Olivia, stop it," I say, using my grown-up voice to zero effect. "Put. It. Down." I try to take the hammer off her, except she's stronger than I imagined and we end up wrestling with it, like, literally rolling around on the grass.

At one point she knocks my elbow with the hammer. I yelp in pain and scramble to my feet. "Olivia, give me the bloody hammer!" I shout.

And that's when she starts running around the garden, mocking me, chanting, "Elsie said a swear word, Elsie said a swear word," swinging the hammer around her head like some kind of deranged cowboy with a cast iron lasso ... and then it happens – I don't know if it is an accident or on purpose – but the hammer flies out of Olivia's little hand and goes straight through a pane of greenhouse glass.

SMASH!

There is glass everywhere – on the path, the grass, on the floor of Green's precious greenhouse, even on his hideous cactuses...

"You stupid idiot!" I shout.

Mo runs out, flapping, panicking. "What the...? Olivia! Elle! Are you okay? What's going on?" She runs straight over to Olivia – who is nearest the broken glass – to check for cuts.

Olivia laughs again.

LAUGHS! Like, it's funny?

And then Sid runs out. "Olivia! Elle! Are you okay?"

"She broke the greenhouse," I say, sneering at Olivia. "With a hammer. I tried to stop her but she wouldn't listen. And then she threw it ... deliberately! It was all her fault." Olivia is definitely in big trouble now. You can't smash a greenhouse without getting it in the neck.

"It was an accident," says Olivia. "I was tidying up and *she* tried to stop me."

"I did not!"

"Did."

"Didn't."

"Did."

"I did not and you know it and you're a little liar."

"ENOUGH!" says Mo, suddenly. I've never heard her shout before and it takes us both by surprise. We stop arguing.

Mo asks me if I'm okay and then suggests we all go back inside to calm down over a cup of tea and a cake. We sit in the kitchen, Olivia and I at opposite ends of the table. She pokes her tongue at me while Mo's back is turned but I ignore her and offer to help Mo instead. I see Sid through the window, sweeping up the mess and Green finally hobbling out to see what all the commotion is about. Sid explains what happened and I watch his face.

Any minute now, I think, Green is going to explode.

Any second...

Any millisecond...

Any nanosecond...

But no.

Nothing happens.

NO ONE explodes.

Sid and Green walk back inside. I hear Sid say, "... so it's my fault ..."

WHAT?

"I was only gone a minute ... literally. We'll get the glass fixed. I'm sorry..."

NO WAY!

Green sits next to Olivia at the table and sweet as sickly syrup, she says, "Would you like a cake, Mr Green?"

"No thank you, Olivia," he says, "but tell me the truth. What were you doing with a hammer in the first place?"

And I think, surely, this is it?

"We were making the Batmobile," says Olivia.

Green nods. "But you do know you mustn't play with tools, don't you? Sidney and Maureen *have* told you that haven't they?

"Sorry," she says. "I didn't mean to break the window."

"Okay. But you must be more careful in the future. Hammers are very dangerous."

And that's it. Olivia goes back to eating cake. Green asks Sid about the phone call from his agent, and I'm ... like ... what the fuck? When I walked into the greenhouse to ask Green if he wanted cake, I got told off for invading his private space! Olivia smashes a pane of glass and nothing? So it's like, if she can get away with Armageddon, then so can I.

I stand up, deliberately pushing the chair back so it crashes to the ground and I say, "Sod this! I'm going out!" I don't wait for permission or arguments and I certainly don't stop when Mo begs me to wait. I just walk out of the kitchen, out of the front door (slamming it good and hard behind me) and away.

Everyone can just get lost!

At the end of Ocean Avenue, I turn, totally expecting to see Mo or Sid coming after me, begging me to go back, to talk about my grievances like an adult, to explain what's bothering me, reminding me about last chances... And I'm ready for the argument. I'm ready to point out the inequalities in the way Green treats me and Olivia and how unfair it is that she behaves like a brat and gets away with murder; to tell them I don't care if this is my last chance because I don't want to live with Olivia anymore! I'm ready. I'm ready for it all...

But no one comes after me.

The sky doesn't fall.

The world doesn't end.

And I sit on a bench near Max's, feeling almost disappointed. This isn't how things usually work and it throws me. Adrenaline's pumping through my body, my heart's pounding and I'm sweating, but there's no one to fight and I'm not ready for a flight.

I still have Mum's letter in my pocket and pull it free. I stare at it, wondering if there's any point. She never replies anyway. But what if ... what if she did? I kiss the envelope and push it into the red pillar box outside Max's Corner Shop, telling myself, 'this time I'll get a reply.'

And then I go back to the Love's and nobody says a word.

*

It's Olivia's bedtime. Sid, Green and I are eating one legged gingerbread people who never made it to Max's, and watching a deadly dull programme about walking along canals with a dog. Green's bending Sid's ear about some family holiday when the girls were little and they '*did the Llangollen*' on a barge and Sid's either riveted or a very good actor.

I'm listening to Olivia's bath water being emptied, to Mo and Olivia marching across the hallway, singing and stomping their feet. Butterflies dance the tango in my stomach to the tune of expectation. And then it happens; the much anticipated sound barrier breaking moment...

"THERE'S POO IN MY BED!" screams Olivia, the original Monster Child from Hell.

Green finally shuts up, and Sid runs upstairs.

Olivia got what she deserved and I try not to smile out loud.

7.

My bedroom is at the front of the house and in the middle of the night I'm woken by noises in the street. Loud, angry voices. Swearing. Objects – bins perhaps – being dragged across the tarmac. Car horns.

Mum and Billy Slade used to argue at night, shouting, knocking furniture over and worse. The first time it happened I got up to see what all the noise was about, but Billy Slade shouted at me to go back to bed. I looked at Mum and she just nodded her agreement. I did as I was told, but couldn't block out the noise, or the fear, or the dread of what might happen next. I was scared for Mum and scared for me too. Sometimes Mum had bruises in the morning. There was a broken chair once and a broken window another time. Mum told me she was clumsy and never blamed Billy Slade, but I did. And this noise now, angry and impatient, reminds me to be scared so I try not to listen and cover my ears with a pillow. I tell myself, *this ISN'T Mum and Billy Slade. I don't need to be frightened. This has nothing to do with them...* but it's as if the noise has woken a memory that refuses to sleep.

And then it stops.

And for a minute or two, there's peace, except the silence is scarier than the noise because my imagination has to fill in the blanks.

I summon up the courage to get out of bed to look.

A defective streetlamp flickers. I catch sight of Green in the middle of the road, wearing the too-small fluorescent jacket from Olivia's dressing up box, dragging traffic cones from the driveway into a haphazard line down the middle of the road. Every now and again, he stops what he's doing to lean on the cones, to catch his breath and shout at cars. Angry drivers shout back and honk their horns. Some of them stop, get out of their cars and have an argument with Green, but he never backs down and they drive away faster than they arrived.

I watch, baffled, until almost the entire length of Ocean Avenue is reduced to one lane. When there are no more cones Green lurches back towards the house. Is he drunk? I've never seen booze in the house, but that doesn't mean he isn't a secret alcoholic. It would explain a lot.

Green looks up.

I dive behind my curtain, hoping he hasn't seen me but when I peep out again, he's still there, looking directly at my window. At me. I smile and wave, then curse myself for being pathetic. He scowls, shakes his head and pats his pocket – the very same pocket my letter disappeared into. I have no idea what's going on in that mad old brain of his and maybe he doesn't either, but in that moment, I know I HAVE to get my letter back.

*

In the morning, a truck appears outside the house and three council workmen in hi-vis jackets climb out.

When Olivia sees them she jumps up onto the window sill, shouting, "Workmen! Look! Workmen in the road!"

Sid tears himself away from gluing a toilet roll Batcastle to see what all the fuss is about. When he does, he sighs and shakes his head and calls Mo into the room.

"Are they going to dig it up?" asks Olivia,

"Who knows?" says Sid, returning to the Batcastle.

Mo appears with wooden spoon in hand, "What's all the excitement?" she says.

"Look! They're going to dig up the road!" announces Olivia, clapping and whooping like she's just seen Santa Claus driving his nine reindeers past the house.

I glance at Green. He is reading a butterfly magazine and doesn't look up. Outside, the men scratch their heads and stare at the traffic cones.

Mo sighs and turns to Green. "Do you know anything about this, Dad?"

"Traffic calming," he replies, still not looking up from the magazine.

"What's that?" asks Olivia.

"Speed bumps," I say.

"Speed bumps!" squeals Olivia. "Amazing. I can play hill rides on my scooter!"

That's when Green looks up. "There's no way you're playing in the road, young lady," he says, harshly. It's the first time I've heard an edge in his voice when speaking to Olivia, and she's not happy. She jumps down from the windowsill to bury her face in a cushion.

Outside, the workmen are stacking the cones and lifting them into the back of the truck. "They're going now," I say, more for Olivia's sake than anything.

Sid raises an eyebrow. "Seems like that was a bit of a waste of council time and money, eh Maurice?"

Olivia looks up from her cushion, deflated. "But why are they going?"

"I think it was some kind of mistake," says Mo, kindly.

"But I wanted to see diggers!" says Olivia.

"Me too," mumbles Green. "Speed bumps are exactly what this road needs."

I look at Green again, but he won't meet my gaze and his face gives nothing away.

8.

Mo takes a reluctant Green to some kind of social club for old people at a local church. I wonder what they talk about, if they fight over Ginger Nuts and steal each other's letters. I wonder if he blocks the path with traffic cones to stop them going too fast on their mobility scooters. I wonder if they're all as barmy as Green.

Mo says it's good for him to have a bit of company his own age, but he doesn't look happy.

I grab a cake from the kitchen and choose a movie – *Hairspray*. I must have seen it a hundred times already, but it never gets old. I push it into the DVD player, click play and fast forward through the credits to Tracy Turnblad waking up in Baltimore...

Sid strides over and turns it off.

"What are you doing?" I say, grabbing the remote control to turn the screen back on.

He unplugs the machine at the wall. "We shouldn't waste this lovely weather," he says. "As soon as Mo gets back, we're going out. Family outing."

Olivia claps excitedly. "Are we going to Legoland?"

In your dreams. Legoland is like, 2,000 miles away.

"Better than that," says Sid. "We're going to…" He does a drum roll with his hands on the table and for a few seconds me and Olivia are completely drawn in. This is going to be good. This is going to be great. This is going to be amazing… "The woods!" he cries, which I was totally NOT expecting.

"The woods?" I repeat, hoping I've misheard.

"Yes, the woods. They're doing a wildlife walk..."

"Nooo!" cries Olivia. "Bears live in woods and eat you."

"Bears don't live in England," says Sid.

"But wolves do and they eat you," says Olivia.

Sid laughs. "No, Olivia. There are no wolves in England."

"There are because I've seen them and they've got bubbles coming out of their mouth ... "

"That's rabies," I say.

"Yeah," says Olivia. "And there are snakes too!"

"Where are you getting this from?" asks Sid, still amused.

"I saw it on the television. Woods are scary."

And although I'm not worried about bears or wolves, I agree with Olivia.

"What have *you* got against woods?" Sid asks me.

"There's nothing to do there," I say. I'm not telling him about the time Mum and 4 year-old me went to the Forest of Bowland with Milo – her then snake of a boyfriend – and how they had an argument and how he left us there, in the dark, no phone signal, no money, no sober adult to reassure me; how I got bitten all over by insects, dive-bombed by vampire bats and how weird noises that we couldn't explain terrified me. The experience will haunt me forever.

"But that's the whole point of today, because there *is* something to do. We can search for fallen rainbows, make a den out of sticks, and see how many different kinds of leaves there are… And look, the sun is shining, the sky is blue. We should be out there, enjoying it."

Olivia folds her arms and stamps her feet. "I'm not going!" she cries.

"And I'm happy watching *Hairspray*," I say, a little less belligerently.

"Come on, kids. You'll enjoy it. There's nothing to be scared of and you can watch movies any time," says Sid.

So I say, "Well obviously I can't, because you've just turned it off. So watching a movie *any time* is a bit of an exaggeration, isn't it?"

Sid looks between Olivia (jaw out, arms still folded, nostrils flaring) and me (a single challenging eyebrow raised), and gives in. Defeated, he sighs, shakes his head. "So what *are* we going to do?"

"Wash the van with the hose pipe?" offers Olivia, hands together pleadingly.

I nod and high five Olivia. She leans into me and giggles. It's a rare moment of affection between us, and Sid smiles.

"You win," he says, defeated.

They disappear outside. I hang back and restart my movie.

Cue Baltimore, cue music, cue Tracy… "Oh, oh, oh, woke up today, feeling the way I always do…"

*

I'm still watching *Hairspray* when Mo returns. After checking in with me she joins the cleaning party. I say 'cleaning', but Olivia is in charge of the hose and it seems to have turned into a water fight. Everyone is soaked through, laughing, screaming and having the best fun.

I resist the temptation to join in and instead seize the opportunity to look for my letter.

The broken greenhouse glass has been replaced, but inside it's still messy and smelly. A tray of tools and dirty gloves sit on the workbench. Cups and mugs, biscuit packets and sweet wrappers litter available surfaces and a butterfly magazine lies open on the seat. A small table is covered in broken plastic pots, rusty nails and boxes of plant food. Cactuses of all shapes and sizes line up in trays on shelves, and plants hang from the roof. Earth spills out of plastic sacks onto the floor, empty jars and bottles and a stack of orange pots in different sizes perch on shelves. A notebook pokes out from underneath a pile of newspapers on the floor and I pull it free, flicking through the pages in case my letter is hidden inside.

It isn't.

Instead, there's a handwritten list of number plates, including the make and model of the car or motorbike the number belongs to. Some entries have a little comment next to it – *High Lane, travelling north in excess of 60mph limit, Potters Road, failed to stop at red light, Seabrook Avenue, tailgating, using phone* – and they all point to my growing conviction that Green is Mr Looney Tunes himself.

I tuck a shiny silver spade into my belt – I don't know why except it looks new and unused compared to the rest of the dirt and rust covered equipment – and I leave.

Green's bedroom is a striking contrast to the greenhouse. His white walls are bare. The surfaces are clinically clean; no ornaments, no clutter, no half eaten packets of Ginger Nuts or cups of cold tea. There's a single bed, a table, a chair and a chest of drawers with one framed photo on top. I pick it up for a closer look. The photo is obviously a much younger Green with a woman and two children, both girls. I guess this is

Green, his wife and little Mo. The other girl looks like Mo, but younger. They are at a beach. The younger girl has a butterfly on her finger and she looks really happy. I put the photo back where I found it and look in the drawers. The top drawer is locked, but the others are filled with neatly ironed and folded old man clothes. Probably Mo's doing. Under Green's bed there's nothing but a pair of slippers. Green's dressing gown hangs on the back of the door. An envelope sticks out of the pocket and for one hopeful moment I think I might have found what I was looking for.

But no... It's an appointment reminder for Mr Maurice Dancer from the COCKLE BAY HOSPITALS GROUP.

There's no sign of *my* letter anywhere and the best I can hope for is that Green has thrown my letter away, unread.

But what if he hasn't?

9.

It's Olivia's day to visit her brother. Until they are getting ready to go I had no idea she even had a brother, but a storm of histrionics about her shoes (she *hates* them), the toys at the family centre (they're *rubbish*), walking there (she's *sooo* tired), and Mo being *a big fat meany* tell me she is not looking forward to it. She even lashes out, punching Mo in the belly. I'm surprised Mo doesn't react to the punch. She just carries on getting Olivia ready, reassuring her Luke is sorry, that he wants to make it up to her, that they'll have a lovely time and so on.

We watch them leave; Olivia crying and kicking off all the way down the road while Mo exercises the patience of a saint. Sid explains to me that Luke – the brother – is much older than Olivia, and because of the family history they meet at a family centre for supervised access. "Luke's not a bad kid," he says. "And Olivia *is* making progress, but it's hard."

I don't ask questions. It's not my business. But I do know how things from your past can play out like horror movies in your head and I feel for Olivia.

*

Sid suggests bowling. I've never been before, but I've seen it in plenty of movies and don't mind giving it a try. We drive in the camper van and park up on the seafront.

From outside, the Cockles Super Bowl looks like a dump – graffiti on the walls, peeling paint, and one of the letters has fallen off so it actually reads Cockles Super owl. But when you turn around the view is endless; just miles and miles of beach and sea and sky. It's like, apart from a few squawking gulls there's nothing between Cockle Bay and the edge of the world. I stand and stare, breathing in the salty air, enjoying the peace. Most of my life has been spent wishing I was somewhere else, but for a just a few seconds, I don't.

Sid touches me gently on the shoulder. "You okay?"

"I'm good," I say. It's not a lie.

Inside, we're met with a wall of sound; skittles being knocked over, gaming machines, electronic jingles, RnB leaking out through the PA and announcements about special offers or a technician call. Sid goes straight to the desk to pay for a lane.

"What shoe size are you?" he asks, loudly.

"Why?"

"You have to wear bowling shoes," he says. "Take your Docs off."

I tell him I don't want to.

"It's not a choice," he says. "What size?"

"Five," I say, reluctantly unlacing my boots.

He swaps my Docs for some ridiculous flat things with softer soles, and I'm not happy. "What if the last person who wore these had some crazy foot disease?" I say.

"They didn't," says Sid.

"No, but what if they did and I catch it?" Because I did catch a verruca from wearing Tanya Brackenberry's Ugg boots once. She said it was karma paying me back for wearing without asking. I said she was a filthy disgusting pig and we never spoke again.

"You won't catch anything," says Sid, reassuringly. And if words aren't enough, he opens his bag and pulls out a can of Sweet Feet Foot Deodorant. He holds it up next to his big cheesy grin, and in this kind of jokey Christian Bale/Bruce Wayne suave and sophisticated voice, says, "I can personally recommend this."

It makes me laugh and melts any reservations I had about the day.

We choose bowling balls and Sid sets up the electronic score sheet. He shows me to how to hold the ball and how to bowl. I watch his ball roll effortlessly down the lane and knock all ten skittles over. Buzzers and lights flash above the lane and a cartoon of animals dancing and cheering "Strike! Strike! Strike!" illuminates the lane. It's cute.

Then it's my turn. I pick up the green ball.

"Use both hands to hold it," says Sid. "Then grip it lightly ... now, stand on the line and let your arm – the one holding the ball – swing behind you ... and as it swings forward again, let go."

I practice the swing a couple of times, without letting go.

"If it helps," says Sid, "imagine you are sliding the ball. You want it to roll in a straight line down the lane and hit the pins at the far end. The more pins you knock over, the higher your score."

I try really hard, but I'm a natural disaster.

I drop the ball on Sid's bag, seriously denting the can of Sweet Feet.

I let the ball go too soon, watch it fly into the air, then land with a thud on the wooden lane.

I forget to let the ball go and fall arse over elbow.

But Sid refuses to give up on me. "Imagine a line straight down the middle of the lane," he says. "Go with the flow, nice and slow and easy. And relax. Enjoy it.

It's not a competition. You're learning something new here, so anything you do is good."

I try again and again and again...

And then it happens! I let go just as the ball comes up from the swing and I watch it roll down the lane towards the middle of the skittles. "It's going to be a strike!" I scream, excited, and for the briefest moment I believe it ... but about half way down the lane my ball veers to the side and only hits two skittles.

I can't hide my disappointment. "That was rubbish."

But Sid disagrees. He high fives me. "That was brilliant! You've never bowled a ball in your life before today and now you're hitting skittles. You're a natural," he says, generously.

I'm so not *a natural*, but it's nice to hear anyway, and I do eventually manage to get 3 or 4 skittles to fall over with one bowl. I'm ridiculously happy when I do and we celebrate these small victories more than Sid's regular strikes.

Afterwards, we sit in the café and have fries and diet coke. Sid mentions Weston College and specifically the performing arts course.

I know why he's bringing it up.

"Do you fancy giving that a go?" he says.

"Why?" I pretend not to know why he's asking.

"Because of your dream to be an actor."

"I wanted to be Mary in the school nativity, not Tracy Turnblad in *Hairspray*," I say.

Once again, Sid doesn't give up easily. "I did a course like the one at Weston," he says. "I didn't know I wanted to act then, but it was so much fun and hey ... look at me now! Star of stage and the Sweet Feet Foot Deodorant Ad." Cue the suave, sophisticated mickey-take again; this time with a dented can. "You don't have to be an actor at the end of the course," he continues. "But we all need fun in our lives. What do you think?"

I think it's nice he cares, but I wouldn't fit in. There'd be girls there who've been acting and singing and dancing all their lives and I'd be the car crash in the corner everyone laughed at.

Sid is still waiting for an answer. "Well?" he says.

"Please can we change the subject?" I say.

He shrugs. "Okay. What do you want to talk about?"

Unless he can tell me when I'm going to see my mum again or that she definitely didn't rob the bank and it was all a misunderstanding, or that they've thrown away the key to Billy Slade's prison cell, then nothing. So I don't say anything; I just stare at my empty coke can and the left over chips and wish I didn't ever have to remember ... or hope ... or feel again.

"You miss your mum, don't you?" says Sid, like he's psychic now and can read my mind.

I look up from my can and stare at him, trying to work out how he knows.

"I miss my mum too," he says, looking into the distance.

I remember him saying she went to Cape Town. "Why don't you go and see her?" I ask. At least he knows where she is.

"I haven't worked in a while," he says. "And flights are expensive." There's a kind of sad, faraway look in his eyes when he says that and I wonder if he's thinking of his mum, imagining their reunion. "But I am saving up," he adds. "And when I get my big break, I'll be on that plane faster than you can say *Sid Love star of stage and screen*."

*

Back at home, Olivia is in a terrible mood, stomping around the house, looking for arguments.

"You're fat," she tells Mo.

"I don't like you," she tells me.

"You've got a smelly face," she tells Sid.

Green retreats to his greenhouse before she has a chance to verbally abuse him. She asks for food she can't have and kicks off when Mo says no, throwing her metaphorical toys out of the metaphorical pram when Sid suggests a quiet game of Connect 4, shouting and screaming about how much she hates playing *stupid* games.

Mo says seeing Luke always brings up bad memories for Olivia, but if we can just get through the rest of the day, Olivia will be fine tomorrow.

I hope she's right.

10.

I summon up the courage to go to the greenhouse. Green is busy rearranging gardening paraphernalia, and without turning to acknowledge my presence, just barks at me to "Get out!"

I refuse to budge. "Not until I get my letter back."

I'm expecting a reaction, but he stops, suddenly, holding his head, a pained look on his face.

"Are you okay?" I say, my mood unexpectedly shifting from bloody-mindedness to concern.

"Of course I'm okay," he says, wearily, sitting down.

He doesn't look okay.

"Anyway, what do you want?" he growls.

Is this a good time, I wonder? But then again, is there ever going to be a good time? I chew my lip, trying to find the right words.

"Cat got your tongue?" he says.

"My letter?" I say. "I want my letter back?" It sounds like a question, but if it is it's more a question of whether Green is okay or not.

"What letter?" he says.

"The one you made me write the motorbike number on. You put it in your pocket."

He looks genuinely confused.

"You do remember, don't you?" I say.

"Why do you want it?"

"Because it's mine," I say. He doesn't need to know any more. But what if he's read it already? What if he's just playing dumb and he's already passed it on to the police and they're busy tracking down Mum as we speak?

He sighs and shakes his head as if the whole conversation is just too much like hard work.

"Well? Can I have it?"

"Oh go away," he says, gesturing for me to leave with a flick of his hand.

I stand my ground. I'm not going anywhere. "Why do you write down car number plates? And slash motorbike tyres?" I say, trying to keep the conversation going.

He looks at me then, thoughtful, as if weighing something up. "Why do you wind Olivia up?" he replies.

"I don't," I say.

"You do," he says. "I see you. I see all your little games. Thirty years on the force, me. You learn to see everything."

"What do you think you've seen?"

"I saw Olivia eating your chocolate rabbit and..."

"You saw her? And you didn't stop her?"

Green shrugs. "You got her back though, didn't you? All's fair in love and war," he says.

I scowl. "I do not *LOVE* Olivia."

"No, but you will," he says. "Because you are two peas in a pod." He starts to rummage through the trays of tools and boxes under his bench. "We all are – you, me, Olivia. We're a bunch of misfits thrown together by our misfortune..."

I came here for my letter, ready for the fight, but Green's not playing and this new, suddenly *talkative* Green is confusing. "What do you mean, *misfits*? And *misfortune*? Mo's your daughter, isn't she? Living with your family is hardly a *misfortune*."

"You know nothing," he says.

"What's that supposed to mean?"

He stops trawling through his trays and boxes and looks at me. Like, stares right into my face, and says, "None of your business."

I almost regret being here, but I'm still not moving.

Green goes back to poking around in trays, moving things, knocking things on the floor and mumbling to himself. He's a mess – mentally and physically – but an expert at not answering questions.

"Are you looking for my letter?" I say, after a while.

"What letter?"

"I told you. The letter you took from me."

"Oh yes, *that* letter. I can't remember. Sorry," he says. "I'm actually looking for my silver trowel, a gift, and I can't remember where that is either."

I feel guilty, but not enough to go and get it. At least, not unless he gives me my letter.

"Make yourself useful," he says. "Look over there." He points to the corner where there's a bin and a pile of rubbish. I sit on an upturned wooden box and pretend to look for the silver trowel in amongst the discarded boxes, bags and magazines hoping to find my letter. I even open the lid of the swing bin, as if I'm going to go through the rubbish in there, except that the minute I do, the stench becomes overpowering.

"That stinks!" I say, trying not to retch.

"What about my trowel? Is it in there?"

Obviously I can't see a trowel, but what I do see are banana skins, vegetable peelings, chicken bones, and all sorts of other slimy rotting waste. I can't imagine why

Green doesn't empty it. He must have no sense of smell whatsoever. People think kids are screwed up but adults are screwed up too. Green is a living example of screwed-up-ness.

"Who gave it to you?" I say, talking about the trowel.

"None of your business," he says, moving things he's already moved; looking in all the same places.

I know I'm wasting my time, but I'm not ready to give up.

He starts on his cactuses, moving them, rearranging them, maybe hoping he'll find his precious trowel hiding in their midst.

"Why do you grow those things?" I say. "They're hideous and spiky."

"Beauty is in the eye of the beholder," says Green.

"And I behold their ugliness," I say.

He turns to face me. "Look, you didn't come for a lecture about cactus. I'm not even sure why you're here. So unless you want to be helpful, you might as well go." Green covers the tray of prickly blobs with a sack.

"Did you show Mo and Sid my letter?" I say.

"Oh here we go again; the letter. It's really important this letter, isn't it?"

I nod. "Can I have it?"

"I don't know where it is," he says. "And if I can't find my trowel, I'm certainly not going to waste time looking for your letter. Now would you kindly buzz off?"

"You're just like them," I say, pointing at his precious cactuses.

He looks at me then. "What? Like who?"

"Like your plants. Spiky."

"Yes well you're right about the plants. It's evolution. Water, food, they're scarce in the desert. They have to protect what's inside from predators. Otherwise they've got nothing. They might as well be dead."

"What are you protecting?" I say.

He picks up a pack of orange pots, lines them up in a deep plastic tray, and puts a little soil into each pot, using his fingers, ignoring my question.

"Well?"

He spins round, almost overbalancing. "Enough," he says, holding the bench for support. "I don't want to talk about it. What's done is done and nothing will change that."

"So, when you do find my letter, can I have it back?" I say, still refusing to give up.

He looks me straight in the eye then and says, "Why is it so important?"

I try to find the words that won't incriminate me, or Mum, but they just won't come. It's pointless. And trying to get sense out of Green is pointless. I realise that now. Coming here was a mistake. I shake my head and turn to leave.

"Lived in lots of foster homes, have you?" says Green, as I edge towards the door.

I don't bother to reply.

"But you'd rather live with your Mum and Dad?"

I turn round to face him. "For one, I don't have a dad," I say. "And for two, obviously!"

"What about your mum? Why don't you see her? Doesn't she want you?" he says, calmly ripping my heart into tiny shards.

I want to defend my mum. I want to believe she wants me. And I don't want Green – or anyone – to think bad things about her, even if I do sometimes, even if he's as mad as a box of frogs on crack. But I don't have an answer.

"Well?" he says.

"She can't." I say.

"Why not?"

"Police business! Which presumably you already know about. And just like everyone else, you've already decided she's guilty."

"I don't know anything about your mother," says Green.

I stare at him. Does he really not know? It's all in my file anyway. Mo and Sid will know. Maybe Green knows more than he's letting on. Everyone said Mum was guilty.

But I can't talk about it.

All I can do is stand and stare, my heart pounding.

Green turns away. "Sorry," he says. "I didn't mean to give you a hard time. There are plenty of things I don't want to talk about." He goes back to his ugly plants and soil and pots. It's unexpected; a moment of weakness, of ... of charity I don't understand. And it blurs the edges of hostility.

"They think she robbed a bank," I say, surprising us both.

Green drops a pot on the floor, but leaves it there while he stares at me, open mouthed. After a while, he says, "She robbed a bank?"

"No. They *think* she robbed a bank, but she didn't," I say, hurriedly. "She's innocent."

He stares at me. Nods. It feels as if he understands.

And then he spoils it. "That's what they all say."

And just like that, we're back to square one; a square with pointed corners and sharp painful edges, totally lacking in humanity. "You don't know anything," I say.

And then he says, "You still here?"

And I say, "I hate you!"

And calm as anything, Green says, "You can't afford to hate me. Because apparently, I've got your letter..."

But I do hate him.

I hate him even more than I hate Billy Slade.

11.

Sid hasn't worked as an actor since the Sweet Feet advert, but when his agent called it was about a new job. I overhear him and Mo discussing it in the kitchen; something about a kids' TV programme called Superdad.

Mo is clearly excited. "You have to go. It's your career ... an opportunity you can't miss ... you're perfect for the role ... think of the money ..." and so on.

Sid is more cautious, worrying about us and Green and being away from home.

They talk for ages, going round and round in circles, about priorities, once in a lifetime opportunities and living the dream, and only stop when I can't stifle a sneeze.

Mo opens the door.

I pretend to be doing up my boot lace.

Mo and Sid both look at me, but don't say anything.

I just say, "Hi!" as if I've only just arrived, and wander casually into the kitchen to help myself to a snack.

They start talking about Mrs Church from next door whose cat died, and how her daughter is buying her a replacement kitten. I don't join in. I just take my sandwich and leave them to it.

In the living room, Olivia is dressed in a curtain cape and black sleep mask with eye holes cut into it. She tells me she's playing Batman Saves the Farm. She's got a whole row of plastic zoo animals lined up on top of a tissue box tower and she's pushing them off, one by one, making inappropriate animal noises... "Moooo, baaaaa, cluck cluck, rooooar," ... and then she swoops down singing dada-dada-dada-dada (etc), picks the animals up and flies them around the room to safety. "Don't worry little lion/giraffe/monkey..." she says. "You're safe now..." Her American accent is even worse than Sid's.

I sit in the comfy armchair, start eating my sandwich and turn on the TV, flicking channels looking for something half decent to watch. I can't decide between, *My House, New House* and *Make Me Look Like a Movie Star*, but eventually settle on the movie star option because the guy who they're trying to beef up is super short and looks like a bag of bones. There's no way he's going to end up on the same page as Zac Effron, or even Sid Love, but it'll be fun to see him try.

Meanwhile, Olivia lines the animals up on the tissue box again, forcing them to relive their punishing ordeal with sound effects. She's louder than before. Is she trying to wind me up, or just absorbed in her own little world? Either way, I let it go for as long as I can stand, but in the end I have to say something to shut her up.

"Sid's going to be on the telly," I say, knowing this will get her attention.

"I know. I saw him," she says, which almost takes the wind from my sails.

"No, you didn't," I argue. "Because he's never been on telly before."

"He has."

"No he hasn't."

"Has."

"Hasn't."

"His feet have and I saw them, so that means I'm right," says Olivia.

Idiot child. "Yeah, but this is *all* of Sid – like he's going to be in a proper programme – arms and head and everything."

"Tummy?"

"Yes, I guess so."

"What about his bum?"

"That too," I say, trying not to laugh. I didn't mean to get drawn in to a discussion about how many body parts qualifies for a TV credit, but at least the animals have shut up.

"How do you get *in* a programme, anyway?" wonders Olivia, now thoughtful.

"Oh, you have to go to a studio, where you act and they film you and then they turn it into a TV show," I say, trying to sound knowledgeable.

"What's a studio?"

"It's a massive building with all actors and cameras and film stuff. It's where they make the TV shows."

Olivia thinks about it for a while and goes back to lining up the animals, but she's clearly still thinking about it because not one of the animals has a word to say and she's very quiet. After a while, she says, "Can I go with him?"

"Doh! Obviously not. He'll have far more important things to do than look after you," I say.

She frowns.

And then, out of the blue, she throws the plastic tiger across the room, and shouts, "NO!"

"No? No what?"

"He's not going," she says. "He can't go."

"But he'll get loads of money and be famous," I say.

She starts crying then. "I don't want Sid to go!"

"Shh!" I say, looking around to see if anyone has heard. I didn't mean to make her cry. "He won't be gone forever, and he'll be famous!" I say.

"I don't want him to be famous..." The crying gets louder.

Honestly? I can't believe her. She wasn't supposed to cry about it, just stop making so much noise and perhaps be a bit jealous because I knew first. And anyway, what kid wouldn't jump at the chance of living with a TV star?

That's when Mo comes in to see what the fuss is about.

"Sid's going away!" cries Olivia.

Mo looks at me.

"What?" I say, innocently. "I just told her about the job. She'd have to know eventually."

There's a ton weight of disappointment in Mo's sigh. "Nothing has been decided," she says. "He has an audition. That's all." She looks away and shakes her head, then tells Olivia to pop upstairs to wash her face. Once Olivia is out of sight, Mo tells me I really shouldn't have been eavesdropping and in future, could I please not wind Olivia up.

"Sor-ry," I say, and walk out of the room and into the garden where the air is fresh and I can breathe without the suffocating stench of criticism.

It's not nice being criticised. You harden yourself to it over time, but since I've been living in this sugar and spice house of tolerance and smiles, I'm going soft. Mo and Sid never say anything bad. They never tell me I'm *a pain the arse* or to *get out of the way* like Billy Slade used to. They never tell me I'm stupid, or evil, a troublemaker, a liar, or a thief, even though I am all of those things. And they never tell me I'm a failure. But now Mo has. Not in words, but in looks and sighs and body language. And when you're soft on the outside, you've got nothing to protect you inside, and it hurts ALL OVER. I didn't mean to upset Olivia. I wasn't deliberately winding her up. It's not my fault she's hypersensitive and over-attached to Sid.

Even so, I sit on the garden bench, regretting my words, feeling stupid for jumping to the wrong conclusions about Sid, and possibly even the teeniest bit mean for upsetting Olivia. I don't mean to cry, but somehow the tears escape anyway, rolling down my cheeks, splashing onto my lap. I keep my head down, in case anyone sees me, and try to wipe my nose on the back of my hand and I wish Mum was here...

My Mum. Stevie Mackenzie. Who still hasn't replied to a single letter.

... When I look up, Green is there, in his glasshouse, stumbling again. He leans on a shelf but his arm seems to give way and then his body folds and he falls to the ground.

Without thinking, I run to him.

"Green, are you okay?"

His face is still twisted. He doesn't answer.

"I'll get help," I say, and stand up to go.

Green grips my arm and shouts, "Wait!"

I shake myself free, but don't leave.

"Help me ... shtand ... " he says, his speech is slurred, as if words are too heavy. I look around for the empty bottles but there are none.

"I'll get Mo, or Sid," I say.

But Green says, "No!" He reaches up to the bench with one hand, still holding my arm with the other, and struggles to pull himself into a sitting position.

As he does this, his foot knocks the bin of rotting food over. The stench and slime of fermented food rot dribbles out. I open the window and use one of Green's tiny trowels to quickly shovel as much as I can back into the bin before we die an early death from poisonous vegetable fumes. I'm gagging as I do it. Even Green heaves. I'm glad when Mo notices us through the kitchen window, and comes out to see what's going on.

"He fell," I say. "I helped him..."

Mo gags too, but takes control and helps Green into the house.

I go with them and offer to make Green a cup of tea.

"Leave me alone," he says, holding his head. He looks grey around his eyes, and tired.

Mo is clearly concerned and wants to call a doctor.

"It's nothing," he says. "I tripped over some rubbish, that's all. Banged my head."

"But this is the third time, Dad. I'm worried. Please let me call someone."

"And waste everyone's time?" says Green. "No thank you."

Mo says she will sit with him for a while.

Green tells her she can do whatever she wants, but he's going to read the paper.

I see a chance to prove I'm not a completely horrible person and grab paper towels, detergent, a cleaning cloth and a roll of black bin bags before returning to the scene of the crime. Someone has to clear up that disgusting mess and even if Green won't thank me, Mo and Sid will. I empty the bin into a black bag and shovel in as much of the rest as I can manage. Then I clean the inside of the swing bin and put a new bag inside – to make it easier to empty next time – and wash the floor with bleach. I move a few boxes around and wipe down surfaces that didn't even have anything to do with the spillage. There's still no sign of my letter (though that's not why I'm here) and conclude that Green *must* have thrown it away. Finally, I carry the stinking rubbish around to the front of the house where I drop it in the wheelie bin.

A good job done.

When I return to the house and tell Mo and Green I've cleaned up the mess, their faces drop. Green struggles to stand, but he's fuelled by fury and hobbles outside ranting about *interfering busy bodies* and how I've *ruined* everything. He checks the swing bin to see I'm not lying. When he looks back at me, his face is purple with rage. "WHAT HAVE YOU DONE?" he shouts.

Mo tells him to calm down.

My heart thumps hard. I swallow. "I emptied it?" I say.

"You stupid, interfering, child! What possessed you?" he cries.

"I thought I was being helpful..."

Green hobbles to the wheelie bins and tries to retrieve his rubbish, but as he pulls the bag free it bursts and his stinking collection of rotten food spills out across the drive.

He is furious. "Go away!" he shouts at Mo, rushing to his aid. "Go away! And leave me alone!"

I run back to the house, trying not to cry, leaving him to swear and knock the fetid remains to the four corners of the drive with his walking stick.

                                53 Ocean Avenue,
                                      Cockle Bay,
                                    MB11 2EQ.

Okay – so here's the deal. You come and get me, and I'll be the PERFECT daughter.

I'll do ANYTHING you want. I'll be anyone you want me to be. I won't ever complain about your boyfriends, or being left on my own while you're out with them, or not having anything to eat, or not having friends home to tea, or having to lie to my teachers about why I didn't have dinner money. I won't complain about ANYTHING. I'll get a job, so you won't even have to support me. I'll support you instead! I just want to know where you are and BE WITH YOU! (Wherever that is.)

Also, I will be a COMPLAINT FREE ZONE.

And I'll keep secrets too...

Because nothing was EVER as bad as it is living here, with a whinging kid and a mad old man.

Please come back,

Elle xxx

12.

Green doesn't join us for breakfast. I refuse to feel bad because it's not my fault he's criminally insane. At least Doc Brown for all his eccentricity did something useful, like inventing time travel. What I wouldn't give to go back in time right now. Or better still, forward to a time when I'm back with Mum, and Billy Slade is behind bars in some dark and dismal hell hole, never to be released.

But instead, I'm watching the door for Green, willing him not to turn up.

"You need a break," says Sid, noticing my unrest. "Let's go for a walk."

"I don't like walking," I say.

He laughs. "Not a problem. We can crawl around on all fours if you prefer? Or slide along on our bums?"

Olivia giggles.

"Either way … You. Need. A. Break." He nods towards the outside, towards the greenhouse, towards Green, when he says that. "We all do."

"Yes, but walking?"

"Okay, so we'll go in the van. We'll go to town and walk – or crawl – along the beach. How's that? Not too demanding?"

Olivia says, "I love walking, Sid." Liar.

I beg to watch a movie and keep out of everyone's way. "I'll smile too," I say, but Sid's not buying it.

*

Ten minutes later, we're at the beach. We park up on the sea front. Olivia and Mo abandon their shoes and socks and skip down towards the water's edge together, whooping and jumping in puddles. Once again I'm struck by the miles and miles of bleak, beautiful, emptiness. I breathe in the salty air and wish I could live by the sea forever.

"Come on, let's walk," says Sid, after a while.

So we walk at the top of the beach where the sand is dry and soft and our feet sink in. We don't speak. Just being here is enough to take my mind off Green and I'm secretly grateful to Sid. When he takes off his trainers, I make a point of staring at his feet.

"What?" he says.

"Sorry," I say, "it's just that I've never seen such amazing and famous feet before." It's my way of saying thank you.

He laughs. Asks me if I want an autograph and I tell him I'd rather have a selfie of me with The Feet. "I could sell it the highest bidder," I say. "I'd make a fortune."

Even though he knows I'm taking the piss, he gets out his phone and sits down on the sand, patting the spot next to him for me to join him. He points his phone at us and takes the picture; then several more of me, posing like Britain's top model with The Feet. And then in his suave Christian Bale Bruce Wayne voice, says, "It's not who I am underneath, but what I do that defines me..." which totally cracks me up.

"It's good to hear you laugh," he says. "And I'm sorry about Maurice. You know he doesn't mean half of what he says."

Debateable, I think, because Green is clearly round the bend and crazy people say crazy things and maybe they can't be held responsible. Except that sometimes he seems to know exactly what he's saying. I look out at the sea, at nothing; a blank canvas, uncomplicated, empty, and indefinable. I wish those adjectives described me, but they don't and they never will because I am the girl whose mother robbed a bank. I am the new girl in school. I am the foster kid. The troublemaker. Unwanted. Always in the way ... and I should be used to it by now.

"He hates me," I say, eventually.

"No, he doesn't hate you. He's struggling at the moment, that's all..."

He's struggling? What does he think I'm doing?

"...and Mo is really concerned about his health."

I want to say that being ill is no excuse, but I don't. I watch the gulls instead, dancing around a useless piece of plastic, attacking it with their beaks and then backing off. They seem threatened by its existence, but it's a lot of noise about nothing. I feel for the plastic.

"Elle?"

"What?"

"I'm not making excuses for Maurice. I want to apologise."

I shrug. It's not Sid who should be apologising.

Down at the water's edge, where Olivia and Mo are jumping over tiny waves, a dog comes along and steals one of Olivia's shoes. Its hopeless owner runs behind, shouting the dog's name – Marley – over and over, but the dog seems to think it's a great game and refuses to be caught. When Olivia realises what's happening, she starts screaming and it's Sid who leaps to the shoe's rescue. He catches Marley, grabs its collar and carefully releases the shoe from its mouth.

I realise then that Marley's owner is Zayna, one of the girls I met at Weston. She's out-of-breath and very apologetic but Olivia is inconsolable; it doesn't matter that her shoe is perfectly okay, that Marley (a golden Labrador) is utterly gorgeous, or that Sid, Mo *and* me all reassure her it won't happen again because Olivia could win Oscars for making a drama out of a minor inconvenience. She is only calmed when Sid takes off his backpack and distracts her with a picnic. I feel for Zayna – she's probably not used to five year-old drama queens so I make a big fuss of Marley, just to prove there are no hard feelings on my part.

Zayna tells me he is called Marley after the dog in *Marley and Me* – her Dad's favourite film – and he's such a sweetie. The dog, not her dad. She wonders if I've chosen my college course yet.

"I have," she says. "Because we did the Wizard of Oz at school and I loved it so much, and then my mum said she knew someone who did the performing arts course at Weston who said it was really good fun ... so ... well... two and two make four ... I've applied for that!" She looks really happy about it too.

"I haven't decided yet," I say.

And then Zayna says, "Let's swap numbers; you can let me know when you do decide, and maybe we could meet up, before term starts? Be good to see a friendly face on day one."

After we swap numbers Zayna wanders off with Marley.

Olivia wants to play a game, so Mo suggests twenty questions. Sid explains the rules; it's just asking each other random questions about nothing important and coming up with stupid answers. I don't see the point.

Mo gets the first question. "If you were an animal what kind of animal would you be?"

Olivia says, "I'd be a tiger who eats Elle!"

So I say, "I'd be a golden Labrador who eats shoes!" but I make a point of laughing to prove it's meant as a joke, and for once, Olivia laughs too.

Mo would be an elephant, and Sid would be an eagle. Random.

It's my turn next. "What's your favourite sandwich?" I ask.

That's a tuna mayo for Mo, a chip butty for Sid and jelly and ice cream for Olivia. Sid has to stop us arguing over whether a jelly and ice cream sandwich is even possible. Surely the ice cream would melt? Never mind how disgusting it would be.

Predictably, Olivia asks, "If you had a superpower, what would you have?"

I say, "Invisibility."

She says, "Flying."

Sid would be The Peacemaker and Mo says she'd like to bake cakes that sell for a million pounds each, and then Sid could go to Cape Town to visit his mum.

They have a little hug, before Sid asks, "If you could star in a movie, which one would it be?"

It's an almost impossible question for me because there are so many movies I would love to be in. It's easier for Olivia. She wants to be *Batman*. She wants to live in Wayne Manor. She wants to drive the Batmobile. She wants to fight Catwoman, the Joker and the Penguin, and squish them into a pie. Mo wants to be *Mary Poppins*. I settle on being Scarlet in *17 Again*, so that Zac would kiss me and tell me everything was going to be alright.

Other questions include:

If you were an ant, what would you do?

If you could outlaw one vegetable, what would it be?

Would you wear your pants on your head all year for a thousand pounds?

It's completely pointless, and even though Olivia is really annoying it's better than sitting at home waiting for Green to go crazy at me again. We're a million miles away from real life.

*

Back at Ocean Avenue, Olivia and Sid disappear into the garden to make things out of junk.

Mo starts prepping sandwiches for lunch and asks me to arrange some cakes. "Zayna seems like a nice girl," she says, casually, while busying herself with tuna and mayo. "Have you thought any more about the acting course?"

Here we go again. I should never have told Sid about that stupid nativity play. I arrange a bunch of cakes on a plate and don't answer.

"Why not give it a try?" continues Mo.

Sigh. "Because I don't have *any* experience of acting or performing or whatever it is they do, and everyone else will be like Zayna. They'll already have been in a school play or starred in the West End or a Hollywood blockbuster and I'd be just a plank of dead wood floating in a sea of drama school luvvies and wannabes. They'll laugh at me and avoid me like me the plague, which is what usually happens."

"Zayna's not avoiding you. And nobody is laughing."

"Not yet," I say.

Mo frowns and opens her mouth to speak...

But I stop her. "Don't! Don't say anything else ... because you can't talk me out of this. It's what happens. I'm bad news."

"Elle, please."

I head to the door. "Everyone thinks so. Even Green. Especially Green. Because look what happened when I did try to do something good. It just gets thrown back in my face!"

I open the door, ready to storm out, but Green is there blocking my getaway, looking vacant.

"Oh, it's you," he says.

I turn to look at Mo. "See what I mean?"

I don't wait for an answer. I push past Green, head into the garden and sit on the bench in the sunshine, sick of people trying to tell me what to do and thinking they know better. Whose life is it, anyway? How would they like being me for a day? How would they feel if other people pushed them into doing things they didn't want to do? How would they feel if nobody wanted to be their friend? People piss me off. Is it any wonder I'd rather sit and watch a film?

"Come and join us," Sid shouts when he sees me.

Can't he see I'm in no mood for junk modelling?

"Come on, Elle," shouts Sid, again. "What are you waiting for?"

"I'm making a batcelerator!" shouts Olivia.

Mo opens the back door and brings out a basket of washing to hang on the line. "Go on," urges Mo. "You know you want to."

"And you know I don't," I say, glued to the seat. Just because they're having a great time with planks of wood and grey parcel tape, doesn't mean I will.

"You can make anything," shouts Olivia. "It's fun!"

Sid sticks two feathers on a toilet roll tube and shouts, "Look! I made an eagle! It's brilliant!" (Which does kind of make me smile because it's so *not* brilliant.)

And then Olivia shouts, "Or you can help make the *batcelerator*."

Sid pulls a face when Olivia says *batcelerator,* as if even he doesn't know what she's talking about, but tries again to involve me. "Come on, Elle. Please join us?"

And even though I definitely don't want to, I do, because I'm in a corner and everyone is waiting for me, and the only way out is back inside via mad old Doc Brown grouching about some nonsense or other in the kitchen.

Reluctantly, I glue cereal boxes together to make four rooms – kitchen, bathroom, bedroom, and living room – and cut holes for doorways and windows. I make curtains out of coloured paper, a little bed from folded cardboard and blankets from an old pair of Bermuda shorts. I use a plastic bottle and lid to make a bath and toilet, and finally a TV from a caster sugar box covered in silver paper. I made a house like this once before, in school, before the robbery. It had felt curtains on the window, a toilet roll chimney and washing-up bottle trees. My teacher – Miss Angel – said it was the best house she had ever seen and she wanted to show it off in a display. I wanted to take it home and show Mum. Billy Slade called it a pile of shit. He laughed at me and watched me cry when he stomped on it with his big black boot. It was the only time Mum ever stood up for me in front of him and I loved her so much for that. But he pushed her over and she broke her arm when she landed. Mum's broken arm is one of the reasons I told the police about him.

I notice Olivia staring at me.

"What?"

She says she wants to help me because I'm *really clever*. Her words. And call me stupid, but I can't help getting a buzz out of that. So I tell her I need a table and chairs for the kitchen, and a cooker ... and a washing machine ... and Olivia gets to work. Minutes later, she's made a rickety table from a plastic lid, four twig legs and lots of sticky tape. We join forces to make a teeny tiny cooker and washing machine out of light bulb boxes, paint the outside of the house white, and make a roof from egg boxes. While the paint dries, we talk about how we could make teeny tiny people – out of lolly sticks, paper and wool – to live in our house. I look around to see what Sid thinks, but he's not here. It's just Olivia and me.

Having fun.

Olivia says, "It could be Wayne Manor ... And the people could be Batman and Robin and Alfred!"

It wasn't meant to be anything to do with Batman, but you know what? I don't mind. So I say, "Yeah, good idea."

"And we should make Batwoman too, because Batman loves her," she says.

"Okay," I say.

And then Olivia says *the sweetest* thing. "You can be real Batwoman though, just like I'm real Batman."

And even though she's five and annoying, I get a stupid little kick out of not being Catwoman anymore. I'm glad no one told her it was me who decapitated her Batman toy.

13.

Sid gets another call from Melissa Martin. He's been called for an audition in Manchester. Today. It's short notice so he's in a flap, printing a script, running up and down stairs, wondering what to wear, agonising over whether to drive or catch a train.

"We can't afford the train," says Mo. "Not at this short notice."

"But I could read the script on the train," he says, stuffing it into his bag.

"If you leave now, you can read it when you get there."

"I know ... but ..." He bites his lip. He's obviously nervous.

Mo hands him a bag of cakes. "For lunch," she says.

Sid won't take them. Says he won't be hungry. Nerves and eating don't mix. He kisses Mo, man-hugs Green even though it's awkward, and gives me a proper hug. Olivia is nowhere to be seen. Mo told me she doesn't like goodbyes so it's not a surprise.

"Good luck," I say.

"Drive carefully," says Green.

And Mo shoos him out the door telling him to break a leg, which seems a little unkind.

We watch Sid climb into the camper van, reverse onto Ocean Avenue and drive off into the distance. Mo suggests we do some baking together; partly to occupy Olivia and partly because she's been promising me a baking session ever since I arrived. Until now, the whole idea of me and Olivia baking together would have been a disaster. But since yesterday and our little junk-modelling session, I've a feeling we might get on better. I go upstairs to see if I can find her hiding in a wardrobe or under a bed, tempting her with the promise of Batman brownies or Spiderman cakes. I look everywhere, but her hiding place – wherever it is – defeats me.

While I'm upstairs, I tie my hair back and get changed. I've put on weight since living here. Not much, but just enough to make me look less like a bag of bones and more like a normal human.

By the time I'm back downstairs Mo is outside with Green. Her face is red and she is speaking really fast. The words come out in a jumble of incoherence... "Can't find her ... runaway ... whadowedo ... wheredowelook and whatifshe's ...?"

But Green is calmer and puts his hands on her shoulders to reassure. "She'll be fine," he says.

They come inside.

"I'll call Sasha," says Mo, reaching for the phone.

"What for?" says Green.

"Olivia is missing," says Mo. "I have to report it."

Green shakes his head. "She's not missing. She's hiding."

"And she can't be far," I say. "I saw her in her Spiderman pyjamas when Sid's agent rang."

"Exactly," says Green. "She's hiding and sulking because Sid's off on a jaunt to Manchester without her. You know what a monkey she is."

He's right. Olivia was beside herself when I suggested Sid might have to go away, and now he's gone. "She'll be scared he won't come back," I say. Being a kid in long term foster care is all about being scared. You're scared in case you have to stay there forever, and scared in case you don't. You're scared no one will like you or that if you like them too much they'll disappear. You're scared of your next move, to some other place where it all starts again.

"Of course he'll come back," says Mo.

I think about what I'd have done in Olivia's shoes. "Could she have hidden in the van?" I say.

"Is the pope a catholic?" says Green, which makes absolutely no sense to me, but Mo seems to get it.

"Of course," she says. "That's exactly what she'd do! There's plenty of room and Sid wouldn't even have noticed." She grabs the phone. "I'll call Sid."

"Maureen, no!" shouts Green. "Not while he's driving."

Mo turns away. "It's all right," she says, in a reassuring voice. "He won't answer. I'll leave a message." She calls Sid's number despite Green's agitation but doesn't get through. "Damn. He's either turned it off or there's no signal."

Green nods. "At least someone has some sense round here."

"I'll keep trying," says Mo.

But Green is adamant. "No, Maureen, please!" There's a look of desperation in his eyes.

Mo looks at him, and sighs. "But Dad, what else can we do?" she says, eventually. "We can't just sit around waiting for Olivia to reveal herself, or not."

Green holds his hand out for the phone. "I've got an idea," he says.

Mo hands him the phone. "What are you going to do?"

"Terrence," he says. "I'm calling Terrence. If anyone can help, he can." He shuffles through some papers on the telephone table but can't seem to find what he's looking for and gets cross. "Bloody hell, Maureen! Why do you have to tidy everything up?"

Mo steps in and calmly finds what Green is looking for – a telephone number. She reads it out loud for Green to dial, but he keeps pressing the wrong buttons. After several wrong numbers, Mo takes the phone and dials. When it rings, she hands the phone to her dad and tells me Terrence is an old colleague of Green's from the police.

"Terrence?" he says. "Maurice Dancer here. Big favour needed. We have a problem ... yes, a missing child." He explains what we think might have happened, gives details of the camper van, and describes Sid and Olivia – making it clear that Sid is not in any trouble – and asks for help finding them. "Mission accomplished," he says, after hanging up. "We can all relax."

But there's no way Mo is able to *relax*.

She closes her eyes and nods, then turns to me. "Elle? Will you come with me, please? We cannot assume Olivia is with Sid. We need to go and look for her and two sets of eyes are better than one."

We go to the play park first, Olivia's favourite place. Mo asks dog walkers if they've seen her. I ask some kids on the slide. We weave in and out of the bushes where Olivia likes to play hide and seek with Sid, calling her name. We ask at the kiosk. We stand at the top of the grassy bank and shout. We stop Mums with prams, old people with walking sticks, and joggers. But nobody has seen a small girl dressed like as Spiderman and it's obvious she isn't here.

She hasn't been to Max's either.

We walk all the way into town and down to the beach, passing more joggers and more dog walkers and people on their way to work. Mo stops anyone and everyone to ask if they've seen "a small girl, brown hair, freckles, probably dressed in Spiderman pyjamas," but still no one has. "Perhaps she's building sandcastles," says Mo, hopefully. We wander onto the beach and pace up and down the sand, under the pier and along the prom. No one is building sandcastles. Mo checks her phone over and over, and wonders if she should call Sid anyway. Or Sasha. Or the local police. Or Green. She looks tired and anxious, and can't make a decision. It feels as if we have walked miles, and my feet hurt.

My money's still on her being with Sid. I suggest going home and waiting, but Mo won't hear of it because what if she's not with Sid? What if she's run away? What if she's playing a rather elaborate game of hide and seek, and she's gone and got herself lost? What if something terrible has happened? Mo's shroud of doubt is starting to wrap itself around me too. Just because I'm a serial absconder who always manages to find her way home safely in the end, doesn't mean that Olivia will. She's only five years old and wouldn't know what to do if she got into trouble.

Mo calls Green. He hasn't heard anything yet and it just makes everything worse.

In front of us, a mermaid statue has been given a traffic cone hat; seagulls peck at last night's spilled chip suppers, while beach cleaners collect litter and rake the sand. Mo and I walk on in silence, leaving too much room to think.

"How long has Olivia been with you?" I say, after a while.

"Six months," says Mo.

"Why doesn't she go to school yet?"

"We wanted her to settle in with us first. She's been through enough."

I wonder what enough is, but don't ask. "Has she done this before?" I ask instead.

"Not this exactly," says Mo. "But she did run off to the play park without asking. She didn't see anything wrong in it."

I remember the many times I was dropped into someone else's life, not knowing them, their expectations, their rules and habits, and how I just carried on doing my thing, until I got into trouble for it.

"She's calmed down a lot," says Mo.

"Really? Tantrums and food splattered walls are the calmed down version of Olivia?"

Mo laughs, but it's a tense, troubled laugh, and her eyes are everywhere, still scanning the beach, the prom, faces, and cars.

"Could Olivia have gone to her brothers?" I say.

Mo smiles and shakes her head. "I don't think she'd want to be with him." She tells me that Olivia was living with her brother Luke and their Grandfather when the grandfather died. Luke and Olivia found him and then Luke went out – to a fireworks party – leaving Olivia alone with the body for two days.

"Two days?!" I don't want to think about what she must have gone through. "What about her mum?" I ask.

"No," says Mo, shaking her head. "There is no one else."

"Is she going to stay with you?"

"We'd like her to. She came to us originally as an emergency placement, but she seems to have settled – sorry, *seemed*. This isn't going to help our case..." She stops talking, closes her eyes, and tells me she cannot wait any longer. "I need to call the police. I should have done it before."

She starts dialling a number when her phone starts ringing.

It's Sid on facetime. His face appears on screen, and with him, Olivia, laughing.

Mo visibly relaxes.

My hunch was right and Green's contact was as good as his word. A police car stopped Sid on the motorway. Sid's phone was turned off while he was driving, so it was a complete shock to discover Olivia, curled up, asleep in a cupboard, in her pyjamas. He wanted to bring her back himself, but when Olivia was offered a ride in a police car, Sid lost. He's going to his audition and Olivia will be home within a couple of hours. We start walking back to the house and Mo calls her dad to share the good news and thank him for his help.

Our conversation is lighter and easier now. We discuss Sid's audition and whether he'll get the part. We talk about his dream to go to Cape Town and spend some time with his mum again. We talk about Mo's dream of owning her own little bakery, making personalised cakes for birthdays, weddings and special occasions. She'd make a Batman cake for Olivia (obviously), a feet cake for Sid, and a cactus cake for Green. We couldn't make up our minds about a cake for me, and we don't talk about my dream. Mo and Sid think I dream of being an actor, but they're wrong. My only dream is to see Mum.

*

The kitchen table is covered with food. Mo's celebrating, but anyone would think Olivia had been away for a week. We're blowing up balloons when Mo sees her through the window and rushes to the door. I follow, realising I too am feeling an unexpected sense of relief and excitement.

Green shuffles past us. "I'll handle this, Maureen," he says, authoritatively, greeting the police driver like a long lost friend.

Olivia exits the back of the car and before anyone can stop her she runs around to the driver's door to climb into the now empty driving seat. She doesn't look at all shame-faced. In fact, she looks positively proud of herself. The policewoman follows her, leans in and suddenly the blue lights go on. I can't see Olivia's face, but I imagine she's pretty happy right now and I have to smile because this is so typical; she runs away, gets stopped by the police, and instead of guilt trips, lectures about personal responsibility and sworn oaths never to do it again, she gets rewarded.

Mo goes out to join them.

Green continues to bend the ear of the policeman and tries to press his little book of car number plates into the copper's hand, unsuccessfully. Green is forced to return the book to his own pocket and stumbles away, up the path towards me, towards the house, grumbling and knocking the heads off dandelion clocks with his walking stick.

We wait for Sid to return. Green stays in his greenhouse and Olivia tells us repeatedly about her police car adventure on the motorway; how the siren and the blue lights went off, how they had to drive very very fast and overtake all the other cars, and how they caught lots of baddies and locked them up in prison... My excitement about her return is short-lived, but when Mo asks if I'd occupy Olivia while she gets on with baking – she's behind on her orders – I have no choice but to listen to these fantasies.

"I've got an idea," I say, when I can't stand any more. "Why don't you play with your farm animals? And I'll watch a film!"

"No. let's play Charlie Chips instead," says Olivia.

"Who?"

"Charlie Chips is an evil farmer who turns everyone into chickens and eats them!"

I'm not sure how to respond to that.

"I'll be Super Cop, who catches you and locks you up and saves everyone," she says, running out of the room.

"Wait! Olivia, where are you going?"

"To get the dressing up," she cries, from half way up the stairs.

This isn't what I had in mind when I was press-ganged into child-minding. Olivia returns with a bag of old clothes and hats and pieces of material which could be anything from curtains to something the Virgin Mary would wear on a night out with Joseph in downtown Bethlehem. She hands me a hat. It's like a cowboy hat only more colourful.

"Wear this," she says.

I try it on but it is way too small and looks ridiculous. So Olivia hands me a mermaid tail and tells me to be Freddy Fish instead.

"Who is Freddy Fish?"

"Freddy Fish is a fish, *silly*, who lets off fireworks to scare children ... and then I come along and kill him and stop all the children from ever being scared again."

"What happened to Charlie Chips?"

"He's been eaten by a giant chicken," she says.

I can't keep up.

"There's no way I'll fit into this," I say, holding up the mermaid tail. "Can't I just be ... Marjorie McNasty or Barbara Badass and wear my normal clothes?"

"No, because it's a play and you have to dress up in plays. Sid told me. And if we practice it now, we can do it for Sid and Mo and Green when Sid gets home from the telly."

Mo pops her head around the door – presumably to check on us. I'm tempted to ask if I can go now, but Mo gives me a big thumbs-up and draws a heart in the air. I don't want to put on a play with Olivia, but it's not as if I have anything else to do so when Olivia hands me an old velvet curtain and tells me to wear it like a cloak, I don't resist. "Who am I now?" I say.

"President Tramp," she says. "And you want to blow up the world, except I'm going to stop you." She puts on an old man's peaked cap and a pair of tights, then holds her fist up – as if she's Superman just about to take off – and starts running around the room, zapping me, crying, "Peeow! Peeow!".

I dodge the peeows and hide behind Green's armchair, but she climbs on to it and tries to get me with an airstrike so I grab a cushion to defend myself. The peeows rebound and Super Cop jumps backwards from the chair and rolls over on the floor. I run behind the sofa, cackling like a witch, about how I'm going to blow up the world, "... and there's nothing you can do to stop me, Super Cop! Mwah ha ha!"

But Olivia stands in the middle of the room and says, "That's what you think!" and starts throwing fruit at me. Apples, oranges and bananas...

"Ouch!" I shout, when I'm hit. "Stop it! Stop it!" I put my arms up to defend my head and she gets me in the stomach... and it really hurts. I cry out in pain.

Mo comes running in and shouts, "STOP!"

We do. Or rather, Olivia does.

"What are you doing?"

"We're doing a play and I'm killing President Tramp," says Olivia. "She's evil."

"You don't throw food, Olivia," says Mo.

"It wasn't food," she says. "It was bombs..."

And I don't know why, but I start laughing.

Mo looks at me and stifles her own laugh. "Please," she said, trying to sound firm. "Both of you, pick up the fruit and tidy up in here. Sid will be home soon."

At least we don't have to do a play.

When Sid returns, we sit down to the mountain of food. Sid talks about the audition. He thinks he did okay, but it was only a first audition so we shouldn't expect too much.

Olivia now hopes Sid *will* get the job and be famous and Sid says he'll buy her a new Batman toy if he does. Olivia tells Sid all about how we did a play and how she saved the world from President Tramp with apple bombs, and how she's going to be Super Cop when she grows up.

Green doles out boring Grandfatherly advice about working hard at school and always telling the truth, and Olivia promises to do all those things.

Meanwhile, she eats like a pig, talks with her mouth full of food, doesn't say please or thank you and never gets pulled up for her farmyard table manners. Instead, they all seem to find Olivia hilarious and spend much time laughing.

And even though Mo and Sid have been lovely to me, I don't feel part of it. I watch them all, eating, laughing and joking; comfortable and at ease with each other, and even when things go wrong, no one shouts, no one screams, no one gets hurt. If Olivia *is* allowed to stay with Mo and Sid, they have all this and more to look forward to for the rest of their lives.

Me? I don't know what I've got to look forward to.

14.

I'm watching *10 Things I Hate About You* when Sid joins me on the sofa.

"Man, it's good to be home," he says, kicking off his trainers, a plate of leftover salad in one hand and two cans of coke in the other. "Want one?"

I accept the coke, but try not to engage because it's near the end of the film and Kat's just about to read her poem.

"I'm exhausted," says Sid. "That was one weird day..."

"Yeah," I say, still watching the film.

"Thanks so much for occupying Olivia," Sid continues.

And then Kat starts. *"I hate the way you talk to me, and the way you cut your hair..."*

"Mo really appreciated your help," says Sid. Can he not see I'm preoccupied?

"I hate it when you stare..."

"She gave you a hard time by all accounts. I hope you're not bruised ... unlike the apples."

I ignore him. I don't want reminding about Super Cop, President Tramp or apple bombs. "I hate you so much it makes me sick..." I say, joining in with Kat, trying to make a point.

"What?"

I look Sid in the eye. "Sorry, but I am trying to watch the film. It's almost over."

"My bad, my bad," says Sid, holding his hands up in surrender.

"I hate it when you're not around, and the fact you didn't call…"

Sid is staring at me. So I stop and turn to face Sid. "Do you think I'm stupid?"

"Stupid? No. Why would you say that?"

I glance at the TV. I've missed the end of Kat's speech. She's in tears and runs out of the classroom into the car park. I turn back to Sid. "Because even after what happened, and not seeing my mum for years, I still miss her and I still want to be with her. I wish I could hate her, but I don't hate her … not even close, not even a little bit, not even at all," I say finishing the speech for Kat.

"That's not stupid, honey. She's your mum. Of course you want to be with her. It never goes away … And I know it's not the same, because I was a grown man when my mum left the country and left me to fend for myself, but I was angry … and upset. I felt rejected, because she put her sister before me. But of course I still love her… just as you love your mum … and your mum loves you too."

*

The last time I saw her, I was ten. She was outside school and at the end of the day I walked straight past her. I'm ashamed to admit not only did I NOT recognise her, but I didn't like the look of her. She wore a skimpy lace vest. Her hair was shaved at the side, leaving a spike of faded pink Mohican on top of her head. She looked rough, dodgy, and seemed to be staring at me. I was down the street when I heard my name and that's when it clicked; this woman was my mother. No outstretched arms inviting a hug. No loving smile on her face. No joy at being reunited with the child she abandoned. Just a tired accusatory look.

I walked back towards her, hoping, but the hug, the smile and the joy never came.

Up close, she looked older, skinnier, with lines on her face and sagging eyes. The butterfly tattoo was gone, replaced with an ugly black skull.

"Didn't recognise me, did you?" she said. "Charming."

"What are you doing here?" I said.

"I've come to take you away," she said.

I should have been happy and I don't know why I wasn't. We looked at each other, checking out each other's clothes and body changes, trying to make sense of the missing years. When I asked her where she had been, she grabbed my arm and marched me away from staring kids and their parents.

"On the run," she said.

"So you *were* involved in the robbery?" Even as I said it I didn't believe it. But why else would she be on the run?

"Christ no!" she said. "They think I was because I legged it with a bag of the money."

"You left with a bag of money?" I said. "Doesn't that mean you stole it? Doesn't that make you part of the robbery?"

"No, well, not intentionally. I went to borrow money, not steal it. But I wasn't gonna look a gift horse in the mouth!"

"What does that mean?"

"The money was silence money," she said. "Because I know who did the robbery. I recognised the voice..."

"Billy Slade."

"You heard him too?" she said.

"Yes, I heard him," I said, but what I didn't say was that I'd also heard him planning it weeks before, with Madman Micky and Horrible Hank. They talked about nothing else and didn't know I used to listen in. They didn't know I called the police one day and told them everything I'd heard.

"So yeah," said Mum. "He shoved a bag of cash in my hand and pushed me out the door. My ticket to freedom!"

"Without me," I said.

She hung her head – the only time I ever saw her look guilty or embarrassed. "Okay ... so I didn't think it through, and when I did it was too late. But I'm here now and I've got a plan...."

The plan was to skip the country and live in Australia with an *old flame* – Dan the Highwaymen, or Dangerous Dan as I liked to think of him, on account of his short and often violent temper. When she told me I was invited too, I started to believe life was about to get better, even if it did involve Dangerous Dan and his mass of stupid facial hair. I started to believe the years apart from Mum were justified and maybe Dan wasn't dangerous after all. I started to believe we had a chance to live happily after.

But then she said, "Thing is, I need money for a visa."

I asked what had happened to the bank money.

"Gone, babez." She stroked the skull tattoo. "On this, for a start. Cost a fortune. And on hotels, B&Bs, you know, because I needed somewhere to live while I thought of a plan..."

She said she was sorry. She looked sorry too. I could see it her eyes.

She said she missed me. Gave me her address and said it was time we moved on.

"This is OUR time now," she said. "Yours and mine..." She just needed some cash.

I stole a pile of notes from my foster family's shop. I went in after closing, helped myself out of the till and posted it to Mum's address. I never heard from her again.

I've been through every possible reason in my head: she's dead, she's injured, she's in prison, she's being held captive somewhere, she doesn't want me. But there's never a right answer. I don't know where she is or what happened after she got my money. I don't even know if she got it. I spent days, weeks, months on end, waiting for the postman to arrive every morning just in case there was a letter, scared in case somebody else got there first. And I've never stopped looking at faces in the street or on buses or trains or bikes hoping that one day it will be her; that she'll reappear just like she did before. I've cried myself to sleep, night after night after night and not been able to tell anyone why. Sometimes I imagine us laughing, being silly, having fun doing stuff together – stuff we never did, like ice skating, or jumping on a trampoline, or eating ice cream and burgers in an American diner, going to Disneyland. In my mind, she hugs me and says nice things. There'd be no Desperate Dan, no Highwaymen, no Billy Slade, no tattoo ... just Mum and me.

The worse bit is the not knowing; not knowing what happened or where she is. But I'll never stop believing in her return.

And I don't hate her.
Not even close.
Not even a little bit.
Not even at all.

15.

I'm supposed to be keeping an eye on Olivia while Mo and Sid get on with *number crunching*. (Don't ask because I have no idea.) Meanwhile, Olivia is lost in her own little world drawing Batmobiles – or carrots with wheels to the untrained eye – on the window with whiteboard markers. She has no idea I'm writing another letter to Mum.

But she suddenly screams, "Ambulance! Ambulance!" and runs to the front door, shouting, "It's an old lady! I'm gonna let her in!"

The doorbell rings. I glance out of the window and see a hospital minibus parked outside the house and the next thing I hear is Olivia crashing through the house shouting for Green.

As Mo and a very white-haired lady enter the room, I tuck Mum's letter in my pocket.

Mo is very apologetic, saying she had no idea and wasn't aware of any letter. She gestures to the sofa, offering the lady a seat and goes off to sort *the mess* out, whatever that is.

The lady's badge tells me she's a Patient Escort from the Cockle Bay Hospital Transport Service and her name is Evelyn. She sits next to me and looks at the Batmobile drawings on the window.

The silence is awkward so I try to make conversation. "They're my ... my erm ... my sister's artwork. Batmobiles," I say. "She's big into Batman." I call Olivia my sister because it's easier than explaining.

Evelyn nods, takes it as a conversation starter and runs with it. "I always wanted a sister," she says. "I've got five brothers instead!

"Ugh!" I say. "That would be awful." And I'm not even joking.

"They were terrible," she says. "Never wanted me to join in their fun. It's probably different these days, but in my day girls weren't supposed to play football and climb trees; not that I didn't try..."

She stops because we hear Mo and Green having a *disagreement* outside the room.

He says he's not going.

Mo says he should, for everyone's sake.

Green says he's not.

Mo asks him to keep his voice down... and so on.

I look at Evelyn. I can't imagine her playing football or climbing trees.

"I take it your Granddad doesn't want to come for his appointment," she whispers.

I wrinkle my nose, and shrug. "Doesn't sound like it." Again, it's easier not to explain the relationships in this house.

Evelyn smiles and looks at her watch. The hallway voices get louder and I wonder if I should turn the TV on to drown them out.

Too late.

"...Because I don't want you interfering!" shouts Green, outside the room.

"But there must be a reason," says Mo, calmer.

"I FORGOT!" shouts Green. "It's not a crime to forget. It doesn't mean I'm mad!"

We can't hear Mo's response.

The door opens slightly, but is immediately slammed shut.

"There's nothing wrong with my memory!" shouts Green. "I wish there was. I wish I could forget everything but I can't."

Again, Mo's reply is quiet and indistinct.

And suddenly, the door bursts open. Green stands in the doorway, face like thunder and hands on hips. "Come on then! What are we waiting for?" he growls.

Evelyn stands up, apparently unfazed by Green's rudeness, and tells me it was nice talking with me.

Green looks from Evelyn to me and back again. "Oh I see. Had a nice little tête-à-tête have we?" he says, to Evelyn. And then to me, "One time. One time you mess up, and they never let you forget!"

"What?"

Mo grabs Green by the arm and tries to turn him towards the front door. Evelyn calmly takes Green's other arm, as if she deals with mad people every day. Then Mo and Evelyn walk Green down the front path to the hospital minibus and help him climb inside. He's still ranting, about being misunderstood and wasting everyone's time, but I close the door.

Olivia comes and holds my hand. "He's funny," she says.

"Funny peculiar," I say.

We watch through the window as he is driven away, and Mo comes back inside. She looks upset, so I follow her into the kitchen.

"I'm sorry about that," says Mo, filling the kettle. "Dad had a hospital appointment. He didn't tell me about it; otherwise I would have prepared the ground. Hot chocolate?"

I shake my head. "I'm okay, thanks."

She opens a cupboard and gets out the tin of chocolate powder. "Are you sure?"

I give in too easily.

"We've been waiting weeks for that appointment," she says, "I was on the verge of chasing it up. I don't know why he didn't tell me."

"Maybe he forgot?" I say, echoing Green's own defence.

Mo sighs. "That's the problem. His memory *is* awful, but I'm guessing he didn't want to go either." She busies herself with the drinks while still talking. I'm not sure if she is talking to me or trying to make sense of things for herself. "He doesn't want to admit there might be a medical problem," she says, not looking at me, "And he just gets angry if I suggest otherwise." She pours boiling water into the two mugs and makes one tea and one hot chocolate. "But what am I supposed to do?" She brings the drinks over to the table. We sit opposite each other.

Mo slurps her tea, and finally looks at me. "I should tell you something, about Dad." She hesitates, bites her lip, and slurps her tea again.

I wonder what she's going to say that needs such a delay.

"The thing is," says Mo, eventually. "I know there's something wrong with Dad because his memory is all over the place and his behaviour is a little – no, a lot – erratic, and ... I know he's been sharp and unnecessarily snappy with you. But it isn't about you ..."

"He wouldn't be the first person to hate me."

"No, no, Elle, he doesn't hate you, I promise. It's just that ... he's been through a lot ... and it's hard to separate his mental health from his physical health. I think we're coming to terms with it now, but it's all very muddled and difficult to understand." She stops again, weighing up her words. And then, "Please don't tell him I told you this, but he was arrested for theft."

"Theft?" I'm shocked.

"They let him off," she says. "He stole some vegetables from a shop. It's not a huge crime in the big scheme of things, but he did walk out without paying. He said he'd forgotten to pay – and he probably had because he's not dishonest – except why would someone forget? It made me start questioning some of this other behaviour."

"Other behaviour?"

"Poor decisions, and questionable associations," she says. "I don't want to go into it, but it worried me enough to persuade him to move in with us. He didn't – and still doesn't – want to be here, if I'm honest ... and remember those traffic cones that appeared in the street the other morning?"

I nod.

"That was Dad too."

I don't admit I saw him doing it. "But why?"

Mo lets out a long despairing sigh. "I used to have a sister," she says. "Alice."

I remember the photo in Green's room, of Mo and the other little girl with the butterfly on her finger.

"I'm afraid she died in a traffic accident. Hit by a speeding car."

I hold my hands to my face. "No! That's awful."

"It was a long time ago. I can talk about it, but I don't think Dad will ever get over it. He has always felt responsible."

"But he wasn't driving the car?"

"No, but Alice ran into the road after an argument with Dad. She was very hot-headed and dramatic; storming off, to make a point. She wasn't thinking about roads or cars or stopping to look both ways."

"So it can't be Green's fault."

"No, but if they hadn't argued, Alice might still be here today. That's what he can't forgive."

The traffic cones – traffic calming, Green called them – the speeding motorbike with slashed tyres, the book of number plates, all suddenly make sense. "How old was Alice?" I ask.

"Sixteen," says Mo. "And I think in some ways, you remind Dad of her. You definitely remind *me* of Alice. And we love having you here, but I think it might be why Dad is finding it hard to adjust."

When I see people who look like Mum, I get my hopes up and feel excited. When that person turns out not to be Mum I hate them, irrationally, because I don't even know them. Maybe that's what Green is going through. I remind him of Alice, and worse, I remind him he'll never see her again.

"And the thing about the rotting food in his bin," continues Mo, "is that it was there for a reason. And that reason was all to do with Alice."

"I don't understand."

"It's a long story," says Mo, but goes on to explain how Alice loved butterflies and the rotting food was for a very rare butterfly Alice was desperate to see. As unlikely as it sounds, Green was saving up to see that butterfly because Alice never got the chance.

"It's taken him years to get round to it," says Mo. "Because not long after Alice died Mum died too.

Dad's behaviour changed and he had a lot on his plate, but now – just as his health is deteriorating – the whole butterfly obsession has come back to haunt him. That's why he reacted in the way he did. I just wanted you to understand."

It explains a lot, and for the first time since I've lived with this family, I feel sorry for Green.

Sorry, and guilty.

*

When Green returns from his appointment, he pushes past Mo and heads for the garden. I watch him stumbling furiously into his glass sanctuary, hissing and swearing under his breath, knocking things over. Is he still mad at Mo or did something happen at his appointment to make him madder? He sits down, grabs a butterfly magazine and stares at the pages as if reading, but his eyes aren't moving. I get it; fury has a way of jumbling everything up in your head till nothing makes sense. It was the same when the morons at school got wind of me being Stevie Mackenzie's abandoned daughter and wrongly diagnosed me with terminal criminality by association. The more I argued the more certain they were I was guilty. So when some teacher fresh out of nappies wanted to know why I wasn't concentrating, or why I wasn't reading the Shakespeare like everyone else, or why I didn't do my homework, there was the answer: fury made me blind. And Green isn't reading that butterfly magazine because he's blind too.

I never thought I would identify with Green, but maybe he's right about us having things in common, about us being misfits thrown together by our misfortune. He messes up. I mess up. We're a couple of mess-ups.

But it's not our fault. We are not to blame.

I tap on the greenhouse door.

"Go away," he says, without even looking up.

I push the door open anyway.

"I thought I told you to go away."

"Yes, but there's something I want to say."

He sighs. "What now?"

"I've come to apologise," I say.

He lowers the magazine and his eyes burn into my soul.

"I'm sorry about the food," I say. "I was trying to help."

"You've got no idea, have you?" he says.

"I was trying to be nice..."

Green shakes his head, as if he doesn't want to listen.

"...But I should never have interfered."

"Exactly. Now get lost." He looks back at his magazine. It's an article with the headline, MOTHS MATTER.

I don't move.

Mo's face appears at the kitchen window.

I smile at her and she moves away. I wonder if I should go inside, but something keeps me here.

After a while, I say, "Mo told me why you got mad when I cleaned up."

He laughs – not a real laugh, but a deep down sneering laugh – and says, "Did she now?"

I shrug. "So I am, truly sorry."

"Get lost," he says.

But I'm not going to walk away from this one. I want Green to understand me, just as much as I'm starting to understand him. I want a conversation. It's not too much to ask. So I say, "I thought butterflies ate plants and flowers and ... stuff like that."

"Mostly they do," he says. "But the rotting food you threw away, the food I had been collecting for weeks, the stinking food I had lived with and put up with, was for a different kind of butterfly; a beast of a creature – the bad boy of butterflies who lives off rotting food, roadkill, dog poo, fish, even rotting flesh; anything that smells bad. They call it the Purple Emperor!"

My heart stops.

Time stands still.

I flashback to that moment in the bank. Tears sting my eyes. "Purple Emperor?" I say. "Tell me you're joking."

"Why would I joke?"

"It's just that ... I've seen one!"

Green drops his moth magazine and looks interested all of a sudden. "*You've* seen one?"

"Well, not a real one. I saw a picture of..."

Green grabs a different magazine from one of his boxes, and opens it to a page with a picture of Mum's butterfly.

"That's the one!" I say.

*

Billy Slade was The Purple Emperor. Just as everyone else in the Highwaymen had some kind of stupid nickname, so did Billy Slade. We didn't know what it meant so I asked Miss Angel, my teacher, and she discovered it was a butterfly. She showed me pictures of a rich purple creature, with black velvet edging and snow white markings. She said it was very rare. Billy Slade was an ugly, scar-faced, bearded, gorilla look-a-like, but Mum was in love with him and explained his butterfly nickname as being more to do with his personality than his looks. 'It's because he's fast and free and there isn't another man like him in the world.'

She wanted to prove her love to Billy Slade.

The butterfly tattoo was that proof.

Eight hours of needle pricks later, Mum went back to The Highwaymen's clubhouse to show off her tattoo. I stayed at the flat with a multipack of crisps and a can of cola. She wasn't gone long and I hadn't even finished my multipack when she returned, red-eyed and angry. She fled to the bathroom where I found her scrubbing the butterfly with bleach, crying, calling Miss Angel stupid, over and over again.

"What are you doing?" I asked.

"Getting rid of it."

"Why? It's pretty?"

She stopped for a second and looked at me. "No. It's not PRETTY. And it's not about purple butterflies; it's about purple drugs, apparently, only I was too stupid to know that..." scrub, scrub. "Stupid. Stupid bitch..."

We were at the bank, asking for a loan to save Mum's relationship with Billy Slade, gang member and local drug dealer, and neither of us knew it was the same day he planned to rob it.

"Cat got your tongue?" says Green.

"No, sorry," I say. "I was just remembering where I'd seen the picture of one of these."

"I don't care," he says. "The point is, as butterflies go, these bad boys are rare. There's a two, maybe three week window of opportunity every summer. That's what the food was for; to lure it close enough for me to see it."

"And I ruined it?"

"Sure did," he says.

"I'm sorry."

Green looks down at his book and the picture of the Purple Emperor. I should walk away now, but I can't. "Why is it your last chance?" I say, not because I'm expecting an answer, but because there's always next year, or the year after. If you want to see something – or someone – that badly, you have to keep hope alive.

Green's eyes glaze over. "You're awfully nosey for a kid," he says.

I chew the inside of my cheek, and watch Green wrestling with his thoughts. I wonder if I should go. If he's had a bad day, he doesn't need me here making it worse.

And then he says, "Alice, my daughter, Maureen's sister, was desperate to see this stinking beast of a butterfly. She was butterfly obsessed – had been for years – and then she saw something about the Purple Emperor on TV or at school – I don't know – and she wanted to see one. Desperately. And every year, it was, *Daddy, can we see the butterfly? Daddy, will you take us to Brackley Woods? Daddy, when are we going?* Because apart from the miniscule window of time opportunity, this awkward creature only shows up in the south. I'd been promising to take her for years, except work always got in the way. You can't just abandon police work when it suits you."

"But you never went."

"We were ready to leave and I got a call. There was a robbery, a bank robbery. The robbers were armed and dangerous and it was all hands on deck. I told Alice we couldn't go. We argued. Then she ran out of the house and into the road. She was very hot-headed..."

"And she was hit by a car."

"It didn't even stop. My Alice, left for dead by someone late home for lunch, and it was my fault," he says.

"No. It wasn't."

"Yes. Because I made a promise and didn't keep it. Police work came first," says Green.

"You can't blame yourself..."

"I CAN. AND I DO. I PROMISED ALICE. SO IT'S MY FAULT!" He punches the bench.

I jump.

A can falls off a shelf and onto the floor.

"And ever since then, even though Alice isn't here, I've been promising her I'll go and see it. I just want to be able to tell her what it was like..." There are tears in his eyes. "And tell her that I kept my promise ... in the end." He looks away, and wipes his eyes.

"You could go next year," I say, trying to be helpful.

But Green shakes his head. "I'm not going to make next year," he says, looking down, grabbing a magazine and pretending to read again.

I don't know what to say, so I stand there, saying nothing. It's just me and Green, alone with the aftermath of his confession.

After a while he says, "It was a stupid idea anyway." And I take that as my cue to leave.

*

I dream about Mum. She's in the Forest of Bowland, alone, crying, but I can't get to her because I won't go into the trees. I'm scared. I call her name and when she can't hear me I write letters instead and give them to Olivia. Olivia runs across a road and is hit by a car. BANG!

The noise of the collision jolts me awake and I sit upright in bed.

"Noooo!"

It was only a dream, but I'm sweating and scared and run to Olivia's room.

She's okay, snuggled in bed with a knitted spider Mo got from a charity shop.

"Thank you!" I say, to no one in particular, and stand there, staring at Olivia, glad she's alive. Glad I'm awake.

And then Olivia moves. Her eye opens slightly and when she sees me she starts shouting. "Mo! Sid! My sister's in my room!"

"No, no, Olivia, it's okay," I say. "I was checking you were all right."

Mo and Sid rush in. "What are you doing here?" says Mo.

"I ... I had a dream. A nightmare. About Olivia. I just wanted to check she was okay."

Mo smiles. Puts her arm around me. "Well I think we can see she's fine."

She guides me back to my own bed. Sid stays to settle Olivia. I apologise for waking everyone up. And when I'm alone again, I realise something good happened: Olivia called me her sister.

16.

Sid offers me the laptop to find out about Purple Emperor butterflies, but as soon as I'm on it Olivia is there too. "What are you doing? Is it a game? Can I have a go?"

I tell her I'm researching but she doesn't know what research is, so I have to explain in kiddie language. "I want to find out about butterflies so I'm looking on the computer because it has lots of information about everything."

"Does it have formation about me?" she wonders.

"*IN*formation," I say. "And hopefully not."

"What about you?"

"No, I don't think there's anything about me either."

"So not everything, then?"

"No..." (Deep breathe ... count to ten) "... I'm looking for *in*formation about butterflies, so I can help Green." Last night's sisterly affection is wearing off.

"He already knows about butterflies. He's got lots of comics in his greenhouse."

"But I want to find out about one particular butterfly."

"Is it Green's friend?"

"What do you mean, Green's friend?"

"I mean, is the butterfly Green's friend."

Can people and butterflies be friends? I suppose in Olivia's world they can, so I say, "Yes," if only to make her go away and leave me alone.

But it doesn't work. "Can I help?" she says.

"Well not really, because this is a one person job." I just want to find out about the rotten smells it's attracted to because I have an idea.

"But I can press the buttons," says Olivia. "I'm really good at pressing buttons. Sid lets me press buttons on his phone."

I'm losing the will to live! "Sorry Olivia, but I have to do this on my own."

"Shall I draw a picture for Green, instead?" she asks.

Sigh. "Yes, I'm sure he'd like that."

So I find her some paper and colouring pencils and go back to my research.

Everything Green said was true. Purple Emperors live in the south of England and by the end of July they will all be gone. NOW is the best time to see one. It's also true about their feeding habits – there is nothing they like more than rotting vegetables, stinky fish or roadkill – the smellier the better. Green did a good job and I ruined his efforts, but there's still a way to make things right. Food doesn't have to be rotten, so long as it smells bad. And if I were to collect enough foul smelling food in time for him to see the butterfly before it disappears, Green and I would be quits.

I grab some of Olivia's paper and start making a list.

"What are you doing now?" says Olivia.

"I told you. I'm researching."

"But you're writing things."

"Yes, it's a list," I say. "Of things I've discovered in my research."

"Do you want to see my drawing?"

Breathe. Count to ten. Smile. "Yes, Olivia, I'd love to see your drawing."

At which point she shoves her piece of paper in front of my face. "It's a mummy butterfly and a baby butterfly," she says. "And the mummy is dead so the baby is crying."

I look at the picture. There's a big blob with wings, and a small blob with wings. I see where she is coming from with the mummy and baby butterflies, but I'm struck by the story she has attached to her drawing. "That's really sad," I say. And because I don't want Olivia to be sad, I say, "Maybe the mummy isn't really dead? Maybe she's just not feeling very well and then she gets better."

"No," says Olivia. "The mummy butterfly is definitely dead, and the brother butterfly has gone to see the fireworks..." I realise she's talking about her own life and I don't know how to deal with that. So I tell her, "It's a lovely picture, but butterflies don't have babies, so it's okay, no one has to cry."

"Yes, they do have babies, or else how do they get here?" she says.

So I tell her what Miss Angel told me about the butterfly life cycle; how they start off as eggs, change into a caterpillars, wrap themselves up in a little caterpillar blanket and have a sleep before turning into a beautiful butterfly.

"That's just silly," she says.

"No it's not," I say, half irritated because she won't accept the truth, and the other half irritated because I don't want to talk about dead mums and crying babies.

"Yes it is," she says.

"No, it isn't."

"Is."

"Isn't."

"Is."

"Isn't."

"It is because a chicken must be the mummy."

"What?"

"If the chicken laid the egg – and that's what happens because Mo told me about chickens and eggs – then the chicken must be the mummy. Except the mummy's dead."

Talking to Olivia is like talking to someone on loony tunes. I can't win an argument with her, so I just agree and tell her she's right and would she mind if I get on with my research, hoping we can forget about dead mothers.

But she says, "Why are you doing this searchering thing anyway?"

So I say, "Because I want to help Green."

And then she says, "I wanted to help my other granddad but he died too..." which just about floors me.

Green was right; we're peas in a pod and for all her irritating little idiosyncrasies and dumb comments, she didn't ask to be here anymore than I did. "Okay, I give in." I tap my nose. "But it is top secret so don't tell *anyone*."

She strikes a pose and says, "My spidey senses are tingling." And then sits down next to me, with her dead mummy butterfly drawing. "What do you want me to do?" she says.

"Think of things that smell bad," I say.

"Poo!" she says, giggling. "Poo is the stinkiest thing."

I write it down, even though I have no intention of collecting poo from anyone or anywhere.

"And fish," says Olivia. "Fish stinks."

I add that to the list. "Nice one."

"Burnt sausages," says Olivia. "And popcorn."

They're not really what I had in mind, but I write them down anyway.

"And farts!" says Olivia, sticking her bum out and blowing raspberries with her mouth.

"What about cabbage?" I say.

Olivia nods.

"And garlic? Do you think that's a bad smell?"

"I like garlic," says Olivia. "But I don't like cauliflower. And onions make me cry."

I add cauliflower to the list, and cabbage, and onions.

And then Olivia starts to get silly. "Bottoms, toilets, Mrs Church's cat's poo ... some dog poo I trod in at the park ... Sid's feet!"

I laugh. "No, Sid's feet smell great because he uses Sweet Feet Foot Deodorant."

At which point, Sid appears from out of nowhere. "Did somebody mention my sweet smelling beautiful feet?" he says, all Christian Bale-y.

I show him the list of smelly things and tell him my plan to help Green see the Purple Emperor and he's really enthusiastic, chipping in with a few of his own ideas about what would smell bad, (wet dog, locker room, skunk, diesel fuel – none of which are very helpful) and then offers to drive us to Brackley Woods to deliver those smells.

"Us?"

"Of course," says Sid. "We'll all go. A family day out. It'll be great."

Just for a moment, I'm back in the Forest of Bowland, alone, abandoned, frightened. My stomach turns over. I was never going to go *with* Green.

"What's up, Elle?" he asks, sensing my resistance.

"Erm ... This is Green's trip, not mine."

"Yes, but you want to be there, don't you?"

Sure, I want to see the look on Green's face if we *do* see a Purple Emperor, but I don't want to go to *the woods* – any woods – ever again. Maybe there's a way out? Maybe we could just forget the whole thing? It was only an idea, after all.

And then suddenly, Sid cries, "Stinking Bishop!"

"Stinking what?"

"Stinking Bishop. It's a cheese. I don't know why I didn't think of it before. If you want stinky, the bishop is your man." He fist punches the air, like he's just scored a goal, high fives Olivia and tells me, "This is going to be amazing. You're a genius, Elle. We'll go shopping after lunch"

His enthusiasm is infectious and for the time being, I resolve to be brave.

During lunch, Green complains a lot. He doesn't want his sandwich. The smell of baking is making him feel sick. Why can't Mo get a proper job? Olivia has terrible table manners. He has a headache. Sid needs to do something about those birds in the gutter. That road they're building in Cockle Bay is going to cause mayhem... His grouchiness almost makes me have second thoughts about helping him see the butterfly. Why should we take him to a place I vowed I'd never go to again when he's so rude and angry? But when he leaves the table half way through lunch and falls over in the garden, I know we're doing the right thing. Mo and

Sid run to help him. Mo wants to take him to A&E to get checked out but he shouts at her and tells her there's no point because he's beyond help. It upsets Mo.

After lunch, Sid takes Olivia and I shopping. You can smell the Stinking Bishop a mile off and as soon as we get it home Green is there, sniffing the air.

"Let me know when you've stopped farting!" he says, and turns to go.

"No, wait!" I say. "It isn't a fart. It's Stinking Bishop and…"

"I don't care if it's the Pope. It's anti-social and bishops should know better."

Olivia giggles.

I try to explain. "It's cheese. It's for the Purple Emperor. Sid is going to drive us to Brackley Woods. We're going to see the butterfly after all…"

Green looks from me to Sid to Mo to Olivia and back to me. I don't know what I'm expecting, but maybe a little more than ... horror?

And then suddenly, he slams his fist on the table, and shouts, "FOR PITY'S SAKE! WHY CAN'T YOU LEAVE ME ALONE?"

I'm shocked. Olivia stops giggling. Nobody says a word. And then Olivia's little face crumbles and she starts to cry.

Mo tells Green he needs to apologise. "The girls were trying to do something nice for you, Dad," she says.

Green clenches his jaw and breathes noisily through his nose. After a few seconds, he nods. He looks at Olivia ... then me, and says, "I'm sorry."

17.

Having added Stinking Bishop, fish guts (courtesy of the local fishmonger), boiled cabbage, chopped garlic, melon seeds and apple cores to Green's compost bin it's beginning to smell pretty bad. By the time we're all packed up and ready to leave, it reeks. Olivia takes one sniff of the loaded camper van and refuses to come so Sid agrees to stay with her. It's impossible for me to back out too.

It's a long drive to Brackley Woods and conversation is almost non-existent. Mo tries to jolly us along with songs and jokes, but no one laughs. Green just looks out of the window and seems sad. I'm nervous, wondering if Brackley Woods are going to be like the Forest of Bowland, if this is all a terrible mistake and it's something else in my life I will live to regret. When the silence gets oppressive Mo turns the radio on. I sing along to the tunes I know which helps to drown out my demons, but Green puts his fingers in his ears so I stop. Mo tells me to carry on because I have a lovely voice. I don't carry on and I don't have a lovely voice.

After a couple of hours on the motorway, we stop to eat the mother of all picnics; sausage rolls, chicken thighs, sandwiches, crisps, fruit, biscuits and of course, cakes. When Mo goes off to buy cups of tea, Green and I sit on a bench next to a play area. We watch the kids playing; climbing, swinging, sliding, having fun. Two little girls – sisters, by the look of their matching clothes – laugh and chase each other up and down the slide. Green's face is like thunder and I can guess what he's thinking.

I ask about the Purple Emperor.

"It's one of the two largest butterflies in the United Kingdom," he says. "And by the end of the month, they'll all be *dead*."

That word, 'dead', hangs in the air.

We sit in frozen silence again, people watching. The two little girls skip off to their car with their parents. More families come and go with their noisy children, reusable cups of hot drinks, and bags of take away chips and sandwiches. Young people, old people, couples, men in suits, teenagers, all talking, laughing, arguing, communicating.

I wish Mo would hurry up.

Green breaks the ice. "How many letters have you written to your mum?"

I'm both surprised and not surprised he's remembered.

"Well?" says Green. There's an unexpected softness in his voice and a kindness in his eyes it's hard to resist.

"Lots," I say. Green tips his head to one side and wrinkles his nose. He's probably thinking I'm clutching at impossible straws so I try to explain. "It started when I sent her money and..."

"You sent her money?"

"She needed it. To buy a visa."

He frowns.

"We were going to run away to Australia. It was only supposed to take a couple of days, but I never heard from her again."

"A couple of days?"

"That's what she said."

"Visas take weeks, sometimes months before they come through," he says.

Obviously I didn't know that.

"How much money did she want?"

"I sent her two hundred pounds..."

"Two hundred pounds!?" says Green, eyes wide with disbelief.

"She didn't ask for it. It was my idea…"

"But where did you get that kind of money?"

I hang my head.

"You stole it," he says, reaching his own conclusion.

I nod.

"Where from?"

"My foster carers had a shop. I stole if from the till."

Green shakes his head. "Silly girl."

It hurts when he says that. I know it was silly. It lost me that placement, got me into all sorts of trouble, and could have got Mum in trouble too if I'd have given anyone that address. I didn't. And until Green, no one knew about it. My foster carers and my social worker at the time thought I'd spent the money on sweets or something.

"And did your mum *ever* write back?"

"No."

"Or come and see you?"

"Only once ..."

He shakes his head. He thinks I'm a fool. And to be fair, I probably am.

"I went there one time – to the address, where I sent the money. My foster carers thought I'd run away because I took a bag of clothes and food with me, just in case. But Mum wasn't there. It was a squat. The girl who answered the door told me she didn't know Mum but people came and went all the time. They kept my letters in case she turned up..." When I say it out loud it all seems so stupid. "But ... but it's all I have – the hope that one day Mum will go there again, read my letters, and come to find me..."

Green sighs. "You're an idiot," he says, reaching his arm around me, and pulling me close.

I never in a million years would have expected or appreciated that hug, but when it happens it feels like a little burst of sunshine through the clouds.

*

By the time we arrive at Brackley Woods it's mid-afternoon; later than we hoped, but predictably – despite the long line of cars, lorries, coaches, and angry drivers behind us – Green insisted Mo drive at a snail's pace. When we do get there, people are already leaving and there's plenty of space in the dusty, bumpy parking area. I hope we're not too late.

Mo starts unloading. Green and I sit tight. I stare out the window at so many trees, big and small, wide and tall, their green leafy branches framed by a lacework of blue sky and sunlight; reminding and reassuring myself that Mo would never abandon me.

When everything is unpacked, I brace myself to leave the van.

Mo carries two fold-up garden chairs and a disposable camera. I follow her, carrying the bin of rotting food. Green stumbles, unsteady, relying on his walking stick. I tread on dead twigs and leaves which snap and crackle underfoot; trying desperately not to crush the tiny white flowers growing optimistically in the woodland debris. My eyes are everywhere, looking at things which *do* exist – trees, plants, bushes – and *for* things which don't. Nerves dance in my stomach. Strangely, the deeper into the woods we go, the easier it is to relax. There are dozens of people here; families like us, casual observers, but people who look like professionals too. Green sneers and calls them the *butterfly paparazzi* because everyone is equipped with either binoculars or a camera and there are plenty of super long lenses, pointing, waiting patiently for their moment to shine. One man lies on his back, with camera at the ready, pointing upward into the tree tops. Mostly the butterfly watchers are quiet, waiting, holding out their stinking offerings on pieces of string, or resting them on the branch of a tree. I notice a whole fish dangling from a high branch.

Green seems to come alive. "Emperors live in the tree tops," he explains quietly, excited and alert to our surroundings. "Oak trees are where they are happiest. They get drunk on oak sap, watching the air-space and attacking anything which comes into it."

"Butterflies attack things?"

"They do. And the bigger the better. They'll even attack buzzards."

I am shocked. I want to ask if they attack people, but don't.

"There's nothing they like more than a mid-air battle. They're thugs, I tell you."

I think about Billy Slade, and how appropriate his name was after all.

"Look!" says Green, suddenly. I follow his eyes into the woods and see a trestle table laden, drooping in the middle, covered with all sorts of pots, pans, buckets and trays of offerings for the Emperor. "The butterfly banquet!" he says.

We wander nearer for a closer look.

Green's eyes glaze over, as if this is his dream come true. "We'll stop here," he says.

Mo opens the chairs, while we wander over to the table. The nearer I get, the stronger the smell. But it's not just the smell that disgusts me; it's the sight of rotting rodents – roadkill – dog poo (I hope it's dog poo) and dirty nappies. I hold my hand over my mouth and nose to block the smell. Green encourages me to tip our own offerings onto the table and to smear the Stinking Bishop on the path, which I do. A vicar in a dog collar comes up to thank me and quietly bless the addition. As I walk back to Mo, I notice rotten banana skins hanging on the tree above her head.

I'm hot and sweaty and feel thoroughly sick.

Mo's eyes open wide and she cries, "Stand still!"

I freeze.

Memories of that day in the bank – the look on Mum's face, the instruction to play dead – flash through my mind. I'm scared all over again. And then, suddenly, I hear the click, click, click of cameras, all aimed at me.

Mo points to my head. "On your hair!" she says. "A Purple Emperor."

And Green is staring at me with the first proper smile I have *ever* seen on his face.

In a moment of crazy exhilaration, another Purple Emperor lands on my shoulder – I can just see it out of the corner of my eye – and then another on my hand! I realise I have Stinking Bishop on my fingers and that's what they're going for.

Cameras snap away.

Mo takes picture after picture and Green is buzzing like a mad bee, animated, joyful, telling everyone he's waited years to see this. I daren't move... but when a dog barks in the distance, my dancing purple angels flutter away.

Someone spots another pair, falling in downward spiral above the roadkill on the table and no one is looking at me anymore. I feel happy and sad at the same time and look for Green to check he's making the most of this moment. He's talking to a woman while a man with a camera films their chat. When they leave him, I notice his watery eyes and go over to put my arms around him. He needs a hug. He doesn't hug back and it's awkward, but I try not to take it personally. We brought Green to see the Purple Emperor and we saw it.

In the van on the way home, Green says, "Alice would have loved that."

Mo tells me Alice would be twenty four now had she lived.

Green shakes his head. "Life isn't fair. Death isn't fair."

We drive the rest of the way in silence.

**53 Ocean Avenue,
Cockle Bay,
MB11 2EQ.**

Guess what, Mum?

I've seen the PURPLE EMPEROR butterfly for real.

Yes, the actual one.

And it was amazing and beautiful and incredible – about a million times better than in pictures ... and even better than your tattoo – except that it didn't have you attached to it...

And guess what? It landed on my shoulder! So if you still had that tattoo, we'd both have had them on our shoulders...

...but I don't bother to finish it.

18.

Mo helps Green have a clear out. She sifts through paperwork while Green ejects broken tools, empty soil bags and dead plants from the greenhouse. All the useless junk Green has given a home to piles up in the garden. Mo adds boxes of old receipts, magazines, junk mail, biscuit packets and sweet wrappers to the heap. They chat and laugh together about shared memories and happier times. Pictures of Alice and his wife appear in frames on shelves in the de-cluttered greenhouse. When I dare to comment that Alice looks like Mo, Green does not bite my head off.

Gradually, Green's chaos turns to order.

Olivia and I watch him light a fire in an old metal drum and throw in paper, wood and cane, dead plants and empty boxes. Everything is burned. At one point, when Mo is not looking he pulls a wad of paper from his jacket pocket and throws it into the fire. I notice the COCKLE BAY HOSPITALS logo on more than one letterhead before they all catch light. Green turns them in the flames, then follows through with pages torn from his number plate book.

"This is your doing," he says, to me.

My first reaction is guilt. "Mine?"

"No, no ... this is a good thing," he says, seeing the panic on my face.

"Why?"

"I'm letting go," he says. He pulls another piece of paper from a different pocket, folds it over, and gives it to me. My letter to mum. "Here. I found this locked away in my drawer. Only discovered it this morning."

Olivia wants to know if Green has anything for her. He pulls out a gardening magazine and tears off the front picture of honey bees. "I kept this especially for you," he says. "Because bees are the superheroes of the insect world!"

"Really?" says Olivia, looking genuinely impressed. "What do they do?"

Green starts on about the various attributes of a bee, but I'm not especially listening because I'm thinking about Mum's letter. I should feel happy to have it back, but instead I'm watching the flames and wishing I had the courage to let go too.

"...And finally, Bees can taste things with their feet!" says Green, which cracks Olivia up.

She sits on the ground with her bee picture and all her bee facts, talking to herself.

Green goes back inside the glasshouse, and rummages through boxes he's already tidied. "There's just one thing I'm missing," he says, scratching his head. "I know it was here before and I know it's not here now...." If anything, he seems agitated.

"What is it?" I ask.

"My silver trowel."

I am the worst person. I took it, for no good reason, and hid it under my bed.

"... a birthday present from my Alice," he says.

The stone ball of guilt in my stomach screams at me, that whatever the consequences I need to return the silver trowel to its rightful owner.

Up in my room, I pull the turquoise suitcase from under my bed. I drag the zip round and open the lid. Inside, are a dozen unposted letters to mum, Olivia's makeshift Batmask, money I stole from Mo's purse and

Green's silver trowel. It's a suitcase of shame. I don't know why I do this, but I do know it doesn't make me feel good right now. I stuff the money and Mum's letters in my pocket, pick up the trowel and the Batmask, and return to the garden.

On the way down, I stop off in the living room and replace the stolen money in Mo's purse, tucking it deep down, hoping she'll think she missed it before. It will be a nice surprise for her. And then I go out into the garden with the rest of the contraband.

Olivia sees me first. "You found my mask!" she cries, running over to grab it.

Green looks at me, a mix of confusion and illumination.

I give him the trowel and tell him, "I'm really sorry," expecting the full force of his anger.

It never comes. He just nods with his eyes, and takes the trowel from me.

Lastly, I take Mum's letters from my pockets and throw them all on the fire. Green called it *letting go*, but to me it feels like betrayal.

Sid comes over and puts his arm around my shoulder. "I'm guessing this is the end of something," he says.

"How do you know?"

"The look on your face."

Is it that obvious?

I stare at the flames. When I wonder if they signal the end of hope I get a sudden urge to dive in and bring those letters back. I want to be the phoenix, rising from the ashes to live my life again...

But no.

I close my eyes and listen instead to the crackle of wood and paper as they burn.

I smell the smoke from the fire.

And in this moment, when everything is lost, and there's nothing else to lose, I realise that the Bank of Hope is closed.

"Are you okay?" asks Sid.

I open my eyes. They sting a little from the smoke, but the tears help to wash away the heat and a gust of breeze blows the smoke away. I smell cakes and bread baking, notice a black bird with a yellow beak sitting on the garden fence, singing its heart out. Olivia and Green laugh about something in the greenhouse and the blackbird flies away. The sky is blue. The sun is warm on my skin. This is family life, with all its ups and downs. This is what I've been missing. There are worse places to live.

And in relation to nothing, Sid says, "You have a lovely voice."

"What?"

"Mo told me," he says.

"How does Mo know?"

"You were singing in the van," he says. "On the way to the woods."

Green emerges from the greenhouse with Olivia. Olivia is still giggling.

"You heard Elle, didn't you, Maurice?" says Sid.

"Heard Elle? What? When?"

"Yesterday, in the van. You heard her singing."

Green nods and looks straight at me. "I wouldn't call it singing," he says.

I brace myself for the barb.

But he smiles and says, "I'd call it a gift."

19.

We are in the middle of breakfast when Green returns from Max's with his paper. Mo makes him a fresh cup of tea. Olivia demands her comic. Sid reminds her to say please and thank you. She pokes out her tongue and Sid wonders out loud what Superdad would do faced with such a rude child. They joke about it. Laugh. Green helps himself to croissants and jam. Olivia would like more juice, 'please and thank you.' Mo's baking alarm goes off and she leaves the table to take bread out of the oven. And Sid brings up the singing thing again.

"You know, if you were to apply for that performing arts course at Weston, your voice would be an asset."

Mo taps the bottom of the bread buns. She told me once they're cooked if they sound hollow. She arranges them on a wire rack, so I guess they do. "Have you ever had any training?" she says, to me.

"Training?"

"Singing training," she clarifies.

"Er... no." Obviously

"We should find you a teacher," she says.

"But I don't want training," I say. "I don't want a teacher."

"Maybe not," says Sid, "but an actor who can sing is a double threat."

"Double threat?" I'm not sure I like being called a threat.

"It's just an expression. It means you're really good at two things."

"I'm not even *good* at one thing."

"And I know it's a big *if*," says Sid, ignoring me, "but *if* you got on the performing arts course, you'd get to dance too. Triple threat."

I'm not going to answer that.

"You'd have a great time," says Mo.

"And it's got to be better than a couple of *boring* GCSEs," says Sid.

I take a piece of toast and spread it with peanut butter and jam. Olivia and Green both tell me it's gross, but that's only because they haven't tried it. I don't care that the jam and melted butter both drip down my chin.

"The late application deadline is this week," says Mo.

"I don't want to be an actor though," I remind them, beginning to get bored.

"But that's not the point," says Sid. "The point is that you have to do *something* and this will be fun. Honestly, Elle, you'll have a great time and it'll be really good for you."

Good for me? Showing myself up in front of a bunch of musical theatre wannabes, embarrassing myself every time I pretend to be Julia Stiles, humiliating myself in front of all the budding Zac Efron's out there. Do Sid and Mo remember what it's like to be 16? They've clearly been discussing it without even asking me and now suddenly there's a deadline and it is make-your-mind-up time.

"What have you got to lose?"

I wipe my chin, finish my mouthful of toast and take a swig of tea. "My dignity," I say.

Green shakes his head and mutters under his breath, "Girl's got a gift. She should use it. Some people never get the chance."

Sid passes me the Weston prospectus and suggests I take another look. I finish my toast, sit back in my chair and flick through the pages. I'm not interested in science and technology; I can't draw or paint to save my life; anything to do with sports is a big NO; engineering, and motor mechanics ... just, no; hairdressing and beauty therapies, ditto; I'm not musical, I can't take photos, and I don't want to be stuck in a kitchen all day. (No disrespect to Mo.) All that's left are the GCSE courses (which I did at school and mostly failed), Health and Social Care (which I could probably manage as long as I don't have to actually *care*) and the performing arts course.

I put the brochure down and look at these people – my temporary family. Mo, Sid, Green and Olivia.

And unlike me, they DO care. But more than this; they seem to have faith in me. And instead of telling me how bad, rude or troublesome I am, they tell me I'm good, kind, and helpful ... and that I have a gift. I think of Alice. I wonder what her gift was, the gift she never got a chance to use.

And then my mouth opens and words I don't expect, come creeping out. "Okay. I'll give it a go." I don't know who is the most surprised.

Sid smiles and high fives me. And then in his phony American accent, says, "We got two actors in the family, now."

Mo claps her hands, excitedly, then wastes no time in calling the college. Meanwhile, I finish my toast and drink my tea and Olivia spills rice crispies all over the table. Sid laughs at how clumsy she is and I can't believe what I've just agreed to. I must be mad, cuckoo, loopy, wacko, certifiably insane. It is the single most ridiculous thing I have ever agreed to, and my only hope is that the course is already full.

When Mo comes off the phone, she tells me I have an audition in September, which just happens to be on my 17th birthday. And that's it. My fate is decided. I am going to stand on a precipice and jump into a pit of baying wolves, hoping I can fly. Happy birthday to me.

20.

Ever hopeful, Sid checks his emails. "Nothing from Melissa. Maybe tomorrow," he says, closing his laptop.

"Wait!" cries Green. "Before you put that away…"

Sid looks up, surprised at Green's sudden interest in laptops.

"See if there's anything about the Purple Emperors."

Sid nods. Of course Green wants to see the butterflies again, reliving that precious moment one more time. So Sid obliges, does a quick search for Purple Emperors and is taken to a BBC local news station where there's a video of Green and the woman he was talking to at Brackley Woods.

Sid turns the sound up.

"…two hundred miles," says an emotional Green. "From Cockle Bay this morning." He points at me with his walking stick. The camera zooms in to show the butterflies just leaving my shoulder and head.

"Your granddaughter?" asks the reporter.

"No. Elle's no relation," says Green, looking around. He points at Mo. "But that's my daughter, Maureen and she fosters her."

Sid pulls a horrified face.

I go cold, feel sick, close my eyes trying to block out the horror of what is to come.

Mo swears and slams the laptop lid shut.

I open my eyes to see her staring at Green, shaking her head in disbelief, or anger, or both.

Green sips his tea and tries to shrug off the consequences of his words. But no one speaks and silence hangs in the air like a bad smell.

"Why is everybody looking like that?" asks Olivia.

Mo snaps out of it; tells her it's nothing to worry about and would she like to draw some pictures to go on the fridge? She grabs some paper and pencils from a kitchen drawer and ushers Olivia out into the living room, shooting looks at Green as she leaves.

"This is awful, Maurice," says Sid, when Olivia is out of the way. "What were you thinking?"

"Look, it's just a video," says Green. "No one will see it."

Sid scoffs, and says, "We saw it."

I look at Green. I don't know what to say. He said my name on national TV. He said I was a foster kid. He said we came from Cockle Bay. You'd think an ex-copper would know better.

"But it's only the butterfly fraternity who'll be interested in this," says Green, attempting to justify his lack of thoughtlessness.

"Well let's see, shall we," replies a doubtful Sid. He opens the laptop again and points out the four thousand reactions, then starts scrolling through the two hundred comments below. "Oh sweet jeee-zus."

"What is it?" says Green.

He reads, "I went to school with that girl. It's Elle Mackenzie..."

"Noo!" I say, pushing Sid aside, staring at the words – *thats Elle Makenzee the girl wots mum robbed a bank* – wondering who would have bothered to write that. I don't recognise the user name but it's hardly relevant. I've been to so many schools, it could be anyone.

Green finally looks shame-faced.

When Mo returns alone and Sid shows her the comment, she can't believe it either. "What were you thinking, Dad?" she says to Green.

He looks down at his hands twitching nervously on his lap, and says, "I wasn't."

And then no one speaks. We all stare at the laptop, each of us alone with our thoughts. I don't know what they're all thinking, but I'm thinking about digging a hole and burying myself so I never have to face the world again…

A siren goes past outside.

Green grabs my hand. "Sorry," he says, shaking his head, like he can't believe how stupid he is. "I should have kept my big mouth shut."

I pull away, and stand up furiously, tipping my chair backwards.

"I'm sorry," he says again. "I'll get it taken down."

But I'm not listening. I'm out the room and up the stairs. Fuming.

Because when I start Weston in September – whatever course I end up doing – EVERYONE will know about me, which means they'll know about Mum, which means my life will be hell and even if this placement with Mo and Sid is the best one I've ever had, and even if things do feel better than they usually are, I'm doomed. I'm always going to be known as the girl whose mother robbed a bank, for as long as I live. I cannot escape from the hell of my own personal Groundhog Day.

*

Mo knocks on my door, doesn't wait for an answer, and comes straight over to sit beside me. I am face down on the bed and don't turn around. She strokes my hair.

"You're right to be mad at Dad. He should never have said anything. He wasn't thinking. And he's so terribly sorry... I'm sorry too. I should have kept a better eye on him."

I turn over. "It's not going to make it go away though is it?"

Mo passes me a pack of tissues from her pocket. "Sid's contacting the BBC as we speak. We'll get it taken down. I promise." She is wearing the ring I stole, which Sasha must have returned. My own stupidity and guilt stare me in the face. I wasn't thinking when I stole her ring. I didn't mean to be horrible to her. It's just something that happens when your mind is tangled and twisted in knots by things you can't unravel. "Dad would like to talk to you," she says.

I pull a tissue free, blow my nose, and wipe my eyes. "I'm not ready to see him."

"It's okay. Take your time. Don't feel you have to come down if you don't want to." Before she leaves, she stops at the door. "But remember Elle, I'm here for you. And I will do everything in my power to protect you and make your life as happy as it can be." She smiles like she means it.

"Mo," I say, before she's through the door.

"Yes?"

"I'm sorry I stole your wedding ring ... I ... I wasn't thinking. I didn't mean..."

Mo comes back to me and sits down. She shakes her head. "I understand."

"No, but it was a bad thing..."

"I forgive you," she says. "You need to forgive yourself."

But how can I? I'm a bad person, like my mum.

"I mean it," says Mo. "The ring isn't important. But you are."

I don't understand. A 16 year-old girl comes to live with you, messes up and tries to upset everyone and everything. She hates life. She hates you. And yet you show her nothing but love and understanding. "How are you so lovely?" I say.

Mo laughs. "I could ask you the same question."

Lovely is the last thing I am.

"Listen," says Mo. "We are none of us perfect. *NONE* of us. We all make mistakes. And *borrowing* my ring, or money from my purse, or *accidentally* breaking Olivia's Batman, doesn't stop you being lovely. You and Olivia are family now. We want this to be your forever home – assuming you would like it to. But to make that work, we need to love and understand you."

No one has ever told me they loved me before, not even Mum, and the idea that this could be my forever home is something which sounds good, but I'm not ready for *forever*. I can't be, because *forever* means giving up on Mum.

A little while later I hear the uneven clump of footsteps on the stairs, followed by three knocks on my bedroom door. Thump. Thump. Thump.

I know it's Green, so I don't say anything.

"Elle? Please don't ignore me."

So I stand and open the door to a tiny crack. My eyes are red and puffy and I don't want him to see me like this. "What?" I say.

"I came to apologise."

"Whatever." I try to close the door again, but Green's stick is wedged into the space.

"Hear me out, Elle? Please?"

I don't have a choice.

He shakes his head, and looks to the floor. "I was so wrapped up in my own excitement," he says. "I forgot to be on my guard. Of *ALL* people, I should never have spoken to that ... that *woman*." He practically spits out the last word. "I should *never* have spoken to *anyone* ... and those comments from that silly illiterate child, telling tales ... and thinking it's funny."

I look at him, torn, my heart pounding, because they weren't just tales. Technically, my mum DID rob a bank. There *was* a bank robbery. Mum *did* walk off with some of the proceeds, even if she didn't plan it ... and that makes her guilty.

Green moves his stick out of the door. "I'm sorry, Elle," he says. "I'm a stupid old fool and I'm sorry."

He turns away and I watch him hobble precariously down the stairs. At one point he stops and holds his head. It's not as if he doesn't have his own problems.

"Green?" I say.

He turns his head. "Yes?"

And I say, "It's okay. It wasn't your fault."

*

I'm watching Dewey Finn (AKA Jack Black) telling the kids in *School of Rock* to, "Give up, because in this life you can't win..." and imagining what school would be like if teachers really were like him, instead of the usual uniform, rule and results obsessed Hitlers; wondering if performing arts will be any different. Every time I think about the course, butterflies start clog-dancing in my stomach. Today, they are paused, by Sasha's arrival.

She didn't warn us she was coming, but I'm not surprised to see her. There's bound to be fallout after the video of me with the Purple Emperors went on line. But I let her in and take her straight through to the kitchen where there are two trays of cinnamon buns on the table, a batch of fruit scones on the side, and blueberry cupcakes in the oven. Sasha sniffs the air with approval, but Mo is clearly flustered. She's busy; too busy to entertain.

Sasha sits down uninvited, so I offer to make coffee and put some biscuits on a plate. Mo is grateful and wonders if I'd also mix the buttercream. The ingredients are all there and I've seen Mo do it a hundred times, so I act like I know what I'm doing. Sasha watches me while Mo clears a space on the side and checks the cupcakes in the oven. Mo finally sits down, making a point of thanking me for my help and telling Sasha how much she can trust me to help her, and lying about my potential as a baker. She also mentions the performing arts audition arranged for September, exaggerates my childhood acting dream and declares my singing voice to be one of the loveliest she's ever heard ... and if I get onto the course I'll learn to dance ... be a triple threat ... unleash my potential ... have such a lot of fun ... make friends ... and so on. Mo talks a lot when she's nervous. I leave them to it. I prefer Jack Black and clog dancing butterflies anyway.

After her chat with Mo, Sasha wants to talk to me. We go to my room. She asks how the Brackley Woods video has affected me. I lie, because I don't want to talk about it. I don't want to think about it. I don't want anyone to ever mention it ever again as long as I live. But it's her job to ask questions and she comes at it from all different angles to try and prize the truth from me.

"Did the comments upset you?"

"No." Yes.

"Are you angry with Green?"

"No." Not any more.

"Would you like me to find you a different placement?"

"No." Definitely not.

She asks how I'm feeling about Weston in September.

"I can't wait." I'm terrified. And honestly? At this point in time, after everything that's happened, I would rather crawl into an underground cave and complete my education in total isolation.

Sasha ticks boxes and fills out forms, and then casually mentions a *residential facility* in the arse-end of nowhere, and wonders if I'd like to go and have a look at that instead.

"Why? I've already told you I don't want a different placement. I'm happy here."

"It's a question of safe-guarding," she says, evasively.

I go cold. "You don't think I'm safe here?" I say.

"It's just that ... the publicity, with the butterfly ... it makes you vulnerable."

"What difference will it make? People will find out anyway. They always do."

Sasha sighs, and nods, and writes something down.

"I'm happy here," I tell her again. "I don't want to go anywhere else."

"But it might be worth a look?" says Sasha. "Because they have flats where you can stay beyond the age of eighteen." She says it, with a kind of happy, excited glow; as if it's all I've ever dreamed about.

"So, a hostel?"

"Well not *a hostel* exactly. It's a secure base from which you can enter the world of work. Think of it as an option, or a half-way house."

"It's a hostel."

Sasha raises a single eyebrow.

And I say, "Well it is, isn't it? So don't dress it up as something else. And you know I don't want to live in a hostel or look at other *options*. And even thinking about it isn't fair, because for once, I haven't done anything wrong. In fact, you're only talking about this because for once I did something right. Yes, me, Elle Mackenzie; I actually did something good, like everyone's always telling me to, and this is how it ends up!" I take a breath and wait to see what Sasha has to say.

... Which is nothing.

She says nothing.

Because she knows I'm right and it's my turn to raise a smug, *I-win-you-lose* eyebrow.

21.

Sid wants to help me prepare for the audition. I tell him there's no point because if Sasha gets her way I'll be in a taxi on my way to some hostel in the arse-end of nowhere sooner than you can say, '*that's the girl whose mother robbed a bank.*' I might as well start packing now.

But Sid sees it differently. "Any day now, that video will be gone, and that'll be the end of it. People won't remember. You'll be fine, honey."

I wish I shared his optimism.

"Let's focus on the audition instead." He reads the letter about the audition requirements, nodding to himself, and then looks at me. "This is nothing to worry about. You just have to sing one song and read one poem in front of a couple of people. They want you to do well. They'll ask a few questions about what you want out of the course and try and get to know you. But if they see what we see, you'll be absolutely fine."

The thought of standing in front of a couple of strangers and performing, makes me feel sick. "I can't do it, Sid. I'm sorry."

"You're not up for an Oscar," he says. "At least, not yet. You just have to be you."

"But I don't know how," I say, biting an already bitten nail.

He grabs a pen from the drawer and Mo's shopping list pad and sits down again. "What songs do you know?" he asks, pen poised to make a list, ignoring my doubts.

"None."

There's a little flap of skin hanging from the side of my nail and I bite that too. My finger starts bleeding, so I suck the blood but it continues to bleed.

"You were singing along to the radio in the van," he reminds me.

"But ..." I take a tissue from the box and wrap it round my bloody finger.

"No buts."

"Yes, but it was *radio*. I can't sing on my own."

"Why not? What were you singing?" he persists. "I'll ask Mo if you don't tell me."

I give in. "Frozen," I say. "But I don't know all the words."

"We can always find the words," says Sid.

"I'd never remember them," I say.

"Okay, so what about other songs? What else have you got? What songs did you learn in school?"

"I never paid attention in school."

"Come on, you must have learned one song!"

"Away in a Manger," I say, sarcastically.

"Any others?"

"All Things Bright and Beautiful?"

Sid laughs. "Any songs which aren't hymns?"

"Old Macdonald had a Farm. Head Shoulders Knees and Toes. If You're Happy and You Know It!"

He laughs again, like I'm some kind of comedian, then tells me he'll find something and scrolls through his iTunes. It's kind of him to want to help, but even if he does find a song, even if I do learn the words, even if I can sing in tune ... it still doesn't stop Sasha from waving her safeguarding rules and regulations in front of us and whisking me off to her *residential facility*.

I make him a cup of coffee and pour myself a glass of milk. I used to hate milk. Probably because we didn't have a fridge and it always went off. Now, there's almost nothing I like more than milk and cookies.

"Let's think about a poem instead," says Sid, eventually.

I reply with, "Roses are red, violets are blue, sugar is sweet, and you smell of..."

Sid snorts out a laugh. "Man, you are killing me today," he says, grabbing a poetry book from the shelf. "But we've got to take this seriously."

I know he's right and I know I need to take it seriously, but I just can't shake the idea that all this good stuff – this time with Sid and Mo, Olivia, and even the time with Green – is going to end. It always does. And working towards something that will probably never happen just feels like a waste of time.

"Can I watch a film now?" I say.

Sid glances down at the poetry book in his hand, but doesn't bother to press the issue.

*

Mo takes me to town to buy clothes for college. She's also trying to help me look forward instead of back. She wonders if I've found any poems I like, and when I say I haven't, she makes a list of poets I might like. I remind her – politely – that we're here to focus on clothes. She steers me into Star Buys, D&K and Sandra's Fashions. I pick a few things I like, but when I'm in the changing rooms, Mo keeps handing me more and more stuff. "You have to try everything," she says. "Otherwise you won't know which is best."

So I do. Tops, trousers, dresses, skirts, jackets...

Mo never once mentions that I have put on weight and she tells me I look gorgeous in everything. I end up with a pair of black trousers, two tops – one plain, the other with flowers all over – and a silky bomber jacket with a dragon embroidered on the back. We also buy ring binders, paper and pens; because I'll need them when I start at Weston.

If I start at Weston.

And then we get take-away hot chocolates and sit on a bench in the mall.

Spending time with Mo is a great antidote to the poison in my life. I slip my arm into hers and I'm just beginning to relax when Zayna and a kid dressed as a fairy suddenly appear in front of me.

"Elle! How's it going?"

"Great! Just stocking up for college," I say, pointing at my bags of clothes and stationery. "You?"

"*Looking after* my sister," says Zayna, pulling a *'help me'* face. "Mum's not well, so I'm in charge for the day."

The sister asks if I want to make a wish with her special magic wand.

"Go on," says Zayna. "It'll make her day."

She hands me the wand, so I close my eyes tight, and wish for the first thing to come into my head. Mum. I linger over the image of Mum running towards me, calling my name, arms outstretched and happy. It makes me smile.

"What did you wish for?" says Zayna.

"No!" says the sister. "If she tells you, it won't come true."

I say thank you and hand the wand back.

The sister skips around me, waving the wand, chanting, "Wish come true, wish come true, wish come true for me and you."

It's cute, and makes a change from Batman and fighting crime.

"I texted, but you didn't reply," says Zayna.

"No, sorry ... just haven't got round to it," I say. The truth is I haven't even looked at my phone. What's the point when you don't have any friends?

And then another girl joins us. Zayna introduces her as Sophie, a friend. Sophie looks at me with narrowed eyes, and says, "Ohmygod! Are you the girl with the butterflies? I saw you on the news."

"Erm…" I nod, reluctantly, and look to Mo for a way out.

But Zayna says, "Yes, I saw it too. That looked amaaazing, and you looked so cute with those things fluttering around you." Maybe she didn't read the comments?

And then Sophie says, "I'm fostered too…"

And Zayna says, "Elle's starting at Weston in September. We met at the open day."

And Sophie says, "Me too! What are you doing?"

I look at Mo. She nods, encouraging me to tell, so I say, "I've got a late audition for the performing arts course. It's on my birthday."

Zayna claps. "Amazing! So that'll be a double celebration!"

"Double?" I say.

"Yes, your birthday, and getting a place on the course!"

"But ..."

"But nothing," interrupts Mo. "She'll be great. So yes, double celebrations."

"I'm so excited," says Zayna. "We'll probably be in the same class!"

And Sophie says, "I'm doing Social Care. But we could hang out at lunchtime or something?"

No mention of mums or bank robberies. And suddenly, I feel about ten times better. I nod, enthusiastically. "Thanks, yeah, thanks. I'm looking forward to it."

Zayna's sister tugs at her arm. She had been promised an ice cream and she wants it, like, NOW! I say goodbye. As Zayna is walking away she mimes being on the phone and says, "Call me?"

*

We return to Ocean Avenue and I start to think seriously about my audition. Nothing seems impossible any more. I practically skip into kitchen...

But Sid and Green are sitting at the table, not smiling.

"What's the matter?" asks Mo.

"Elle's gone viral!" he says.

He turns his laptop to face us.

There's now film of me on You Tube too, in Brackley Woods with Purple Emperors on my hand, head and shoulder, and I'm laughing, happy. Cameras all around me are clicking away. It's 2.36 minutes of footage, with over a million views already. If you Google 'Girl with Purple Emperor' there are dozens and dozens of results. I'm everywhere – Instagram, Tumbler, Tik Tok – only this time, it's just me and Green is nowhere to be seen.

If you looked at Mo or Sid, you'd think someone had died.

Eventually, Sid says, "Read the comments." He opens one of the videos on YouTube and scrolls down the page to a very public conversation between idiots.

'Thats the girl wot robbed a bank'
'She robbed a bank? Hillarius!'
'No, was her mum wot robbed it.'
'She went to my school ...'

There's more, but I can't read on. It's too horrible. Mo puts her arm around me and tells me she'll report this too. "We'll get it taken down, Elle," she says.

But you can't take down the whole internet. And even if some people ignore the comments, it doesn't mean that everybody will. There's always one; at least one.

And just like that, I'm back to hating my life.

22.

We're all in the kitchen, eating breakfast, when there is a knock on the door.

Sid goes to answer and almost immediately we hear his raised voice telling whoever it is, "No! Absolutely not!"

The door slams and Sid returns, face like thunder.

The caller knocks again

"Do not answer," says Sid, forcefully, to no one in particular, but I see him look at Mo, shake his head and whisper. "Don't ask."

"Who is it?" asks Olivia.

Mo stands and immediately busies Olivia out of the room with the promise of jammy doughnuts for Batman if they could just go and check on something together upstairs. Olivia falls for it – of course she does – and she and Mo run upstairs, giggling.

The knocking continues. Sid tries to busy himself making a cup of tea, but he is clearly distracted and doesn't look what he is doing. He misses his cup, spills boiling water over the surface and swears repeatedly as he mops it up with paper towels.

I can't help myself. "Who *is* it?"

Sid stops mopping, takes a breath and sits across the table from me. He holds my hand and goes to speak but the words don't come. I think the worst. *They've found Mum. She's dead. I'll never see her again.*

"Tell me," I beg. "Please." Because I'd rather know than not know.

Sid chews his lip, nods and then reluctantly explains. "It's a reporter, I'm afraid. She wants to interview you about the butterfly; wants your reaction to seeing it. And a photo. She wants a photo of you."

I feel sick. Don't know what to say. But I don't have to say anything because Sid's got my back.

"It's okay," he says. "I told her to get lost."

But she's still there, hammering on the door and now shouting through the letterbox. "One photo … just a few words … open the door…"

Sid bangs his fist on the table. "That's it! I'm calling the police," he says.

I don't know whether to feel happy or not.

He looks at me, apologetically. "And I guess I'll need to call Sasha too," he says, who is the last person I need.

*

Sasha turns up with two policemen. The reporter – now apparently with a photographer – is 'moved on'. Sasha comes inside while the police keep guard outside in their car. Green takes Olivia to meet them, so at least someone is happy.

Sasha pulls out the file with my name on and puts it on the table. She's seen all the footage of me with the butterfly, read the troll comments, and of course she's not happy.

"I've started the ball rolling with the alternative placement for Elle…"

"I'm sure that's not necessary," says Mo.

Sasha produces some glossy leaflets inside with 'HOME from HOME, THE RESIDENTIAL CARE GROUP', printed on the front. She hands them to Mo.

"I've spoken to the manager at this place and they would be very happy to take Elle at a moment's notice."

I'm screaming in my head, *DON'T LET ME GO THERE*!

In real life, I'm quiet, bewildered and empty.

Mo doesn't even look at the leaflets; just pushes them back across the table, telling Sasha there really isn't any need.

"Please let me finish," says Sasha, pointedly. "They would be very happy to take Elle *if* the need arises."

"I promise it won't," says Mo.

"But we *are* looking at safeguarding issues, Mo, and it may be out of our hands."

Mo folds her arms. "Elle is perfectly happy here. We want her to stay, and we're offering Elle a permanent home. Surely, that should be the deciding factor?"

I could hug Mo for this. Seriously, never before have I felt such an overwhelming sense of gratitude that it's made me want to hug someone! I don't actually hug her because Sasha is there being all efficient and business-like and a hug seems out of place, but I do manage to flash Mo a finger and thumb love-heart.

Mo smiles warmly, wrinkles her nose and nods. She's got my back too.

Sasha closes her folder and stands. "I understand how you feel and I will do my best to support you, but in the meantime, please do look at these." She points to the HOME from HOME leaflets. "They have a lot to offer."

Mo turns to me. "We'll fight this," she says. "You've always got a home here."

And Sasha adds, "Yes, but Elle? You need to keep out of trouble..."

I want to remind her that I *have* kept out of trouble.

But what's the point?

It doesn't matter what I do because nothing ever changes.

23.

I didn't slept well. My dreams were a jumble of butterflies, Mum, Mo, policemen and hostels. I did something terrible – I don't know what – and always ended up being pursued by shadows. I don't know who or what the shadows were but they wanted to fight and all I wanted to do is run away. I woke up tangled in sheets, not knowing where I was. And the real shadows – the ones on my floor, my bed and my ceiling, cast by street lights – scared me.

And now, morning; a new day and I'm already exhausted.

Downstairs, Sid is dancing around the kitchen, singing. "You've got to have a dream … If you don't have a dream, how you going to make your dream come true?" which feels kind of ironic after my nightmare of a night. He does at least stop singing when he sees my long face, although he can't seem to stop bouncing around like a demented kangaroo, covering the table with bread and spreads, cereal and milk, and an unnecessary amount of cutlery.

I yawn, smile – ingenuously – and put bread in the toaster, wishing he'd turn it down a notch or two.

Green is trying to read the paper, but I notice him glance at Sid and shake his head, as if he too is finding Sid's high spirits a little tiresome. Mo is busy weighing ingredients for her next bake, but she too has a smile hovering on her lips, like she is fit to burst any second. Olivia isn't down yet, and she's usually up before me.

My toast pops up. I grab a plate, the peanut butter and some jam, and sit at the table trying to ignore the world.

Mo can't contain herself any longer. "We've got some good news," she says, clapping her floured hands excitedly, creating a cloud effect mid-air.

Has Sasha given up on her ridiculous dream of exiling me to HOME from HOME? If not, I don't want to know.

"Remember that TV part Sid was up for?" says Mo.

How could I forget?

"Well…" says Mo.

"I GOT A RECALL!" says Sid, punching the air, over and over. "Yes! Yes! Yes!"

"Melissa phoned and they need Sid to go back for a second audition, tomorrow," says Mo. "Which means they *really* liked him and he is one step nearer to getting the job."

"Congratulations," I say. I mean it too. I am not *such* a miserable loser that I don't *try* to look happy for Sid.

"I haven't actually got it … yet," says Sid, "But they're only recalling two of us, so I'm in with a good chance."

"Exciting isn't it?" says Mo.

And yes, of course it is. It's really exciting, for Sid. "But does Olivia know?" I ask. "Is that why she's not here?"

I can tell by the look on Sid's face the answer is yes.

"She's not happy," grumbles Green, spitting cereal as he speaks.

"But she'll come round to the idea," says Sid. "*If* I get it. And it's still a big *if.*"

When I finish my toast and Olivia still hasn't appeared, I go to her room. I might have had a bad night, but Sid going off to film Superdad is a waking nightmare for Olivia and I feel sorry for her. I know what it's like to miss someone you love.

I find her sitting on the floor with her spider toy, tying its legs in knots. "Go away!" she says. "I don't want you here."

I sit next to her.

"I said, GO AWAY!" She turns away to face the wall and folds her arms.

"Aww, come on, Olivia. Sid hasn't even got the job yet and anyway, I thought you didn't mind."

"But what if he does and he's never here?" she says, still facing the wall.

"Then it'll be fun watching him on TV," I say. "And he'll still be here at weekends."

"But what about the other days? Monday, Tuesday, Friday and Wednesday?"

I wonder what happened to Thursday, but decide not to mention it. "Well, *I'll* still be here," fingers crossed, "and *I'll* play with you." I put her eye mask on, grab her dressing gown and wrap it around my shoulders like a cape, and strike a super-hero pose.

"What are you doing?" she says.

"I'm Super Elle!" I say, in my own phony American voice. "And I've come to save the day!"

She doesn't even smile.

I look in the mirror and straighten the eye mask. "And anyway, you'll be starting school in September…"

"I don't want to go to school."

"Yes you do. Of course you do. And you're going to love it there, and all your new friends are going to be, like, '*is your dad really Superdad?*' And '*can I have your autograph?*' And '*can I come to tea?*' which Mo is absolutely going to love because she'll be able to make even more cakes, which will make all the kids want to keep coming back, and of course they're going to love you too," I say, "because who wouldn't? I mean, you're awesome. You're Super Girl. For real..."

"How do you know?" she says, when I finally shut up.

"Well, because … erm ... because I've been to loads of schools, so I'm kind of a school expert. People often ask my advice about things like this..."

She thinks about it for a while, and then says, "Will you play with me after school? And all my new friends?"

"Of course!" I lie.

"Before school?"

"Sure will."

"Will you play super heroes?"

"Absolutely!" I brush imaginary dust off my Super Elle dressing gown cape.

"Will you play super heroes *now*?"

Sigh. I suppose I asked for this. And it's not as if I haven't already watched every film in Mo and Sid's collection at least once, so I agree.

"And I can be Batman?"

"Wouldn't have it any other way."

"But you have to be Robin. We're the good guys, okay?" She leans forward and takes the mask off me. "And you can't wear that either." She points at the dressing gown.

"No problem," I say, untying it and laying it on her bed. I can't back out now.

"At the park…"

"Erm… I don't think we can go..." But Olivia is already on her way down stairs.

When we arrive in the kitchen, the table is littered with bank statements, receipts and bits of paper. Mo and Sid are deep in conversation. I try to steer Olivia away into the living room, so as not to interrupt, but she's not having it. She wants to go to the park and nothing's going to stop her asking.

Mo isn't sure, but Sid's all for it.

"Why not?" he says. "I think we can trust Elle to look after Olivia for half an hour, can't we? And it'll give us some time to sort this out," he says, pointing at the paperwork.

Mo bites her lip and looks from me to Olivia. I can almost see the thought process ... *Elle hasn't run away yet ... but Olivia can be hard work ... what would Sasha say?* She's obviously not keen on the idea.

And then Green chips in with, "They could pick up my paper on the way home. I'm not feeling too good today."

"And my comic?" says Olivia.

Mo looks at Sid for support.

"I've told you what I think," he says, shrugging.

Mo sighs. "Okay. You can go. But only an hour and then come straight back home. Do you understand?"

Olivia cheers.

"Do. You. Understand?" repeats Mo.

I nod. Olivia is already in the hall putting her shoes on.

As we leave the house, Green shouts, "And don't forget my paper!"

We play Batman and Robin on the swings, the roundabout and the slide. This mainly consists of Olivia shouting, "The city needs me!" and "Let's rattle some cages!" and me running around behind her, shouting things like, "Look out Batman!" and "To the Batmobile!" I get some funny looks, but I don't care. Olivia is happy and to be honest it's kind of fun, in a silly way.

And then, long before our time is up, Olivia tells me she needs a wee. I take her to the toilets in the park, but they have been boarded up and Olivia starts jumping up and down with her legs crossed like she's going to wet her pants any minute.

"I'm desperate," she whines.

"Why didn't you go before we left the house?" I say, pointlessly.

"Because I didn't want to go then," she says.

I look for a handy bush she could squat behind, but she absolutely refuses to have a wee where someone might see her and judging by her agonised whining I doubt we'll make it back to Ocean Avenue in time. Town is nearer.

"Could you make it to Maccy's where there are some *big girl toilets*?" I ask.

She nods emphatically. "Yes, yes please, please, please. Because I like it there. And they do happy food."

"We're not buying anything," I say. "And you have to behave." I'm very firm about it.

So Olivia slips her hand into mine and we walk very quickly towards Maccy's.

I'm trying to be cheerful and positive and Olivia hardly whines at all. The only problem we face is crossing the busy road. If I was on my own I'd take a chance dodging cars, but I've got Green's voice on loop in my head ... 'Life isn't fair. Death isn't fair' ... and we need to wait for the *green* man. Meanwhile, I've got a desperate Olivia tugging at my arm telling me she can't hold it, the slowest green man in the history of time, the dread of having to deal with wet pants and a crying kid... and it's all starting to stress me out. Should I chance it? Should I wait? I don't know. So I'm dithering and when there's a gap in the traffic I'm just about to run...

Except ...

At that exact moment a motorbike comes roaring up the road.

A Harley. Just like the one Billy Slade used to ride, and it thunders to a stop outside McDonald's in the disabled parking bay. I can't help but stare at the bike; at the rider climbing off. And in one of those filmic moments, when he removes his helmet a mass of golden hair flops over his shoulders. He shakes his hair free, turns round, and as he does...

I realise HE is a SHE

And 'SHE' is my mum.

My eyes fall out of their sockets.

My jaw hits the ground.

Olivia whines. "I need a wee, Elle. I'm really desperate."

And I don't know what to do. Should I wait for the next green man and let her pee herself? Should I call over to Mum? Should I take my chances with the traffic? My body makes the decision for me. My legs are two solid concrete blocks, rooted to the spot. I can't move.

Can't think.

Can't speak.

Can't stop staring.

Can't breathe.

I watch Mum disappear into Maccy's.

In my head, I'm running in after her and she's hugging me and drowning me in kisses and laughter, making up for the missing eight years.

"Elle!" shouts Olivia, pulling me back to earth. "I really really need a wee!" Her legs are crossed, her face is agony and any second from now she's going to wet herself. So I stop over-thinking it, grab her hand and walk into the road, dodging cars and a bus and a cyclist who shouts at us, but somehow we make it to the other side and we're just metres away from Mum – MY MUM – queuing at the counter in McDonald's, as if this is a perfectly ordinary, normal day.

I tell Olivia to go inside and find the loos. "I'll wait here," I say. I need time to gather my thoughts, and plan, because one thing I do know is that Olivia must NOT – absolutely MUST NOT – know about Mum. If she did she'd ask a hundred awkward questions, tell Mo and Sid who'd tell Sasha, who'd tell the police … and my life would be over.

I look through the window.

Olivia disappears into the toilets.

Mum's at the front of the queue now, ordering.

Should I go in and speak to her while Olivia is out of the way? What would I say? Or should I wait for her to see me? My heart is beating hard. My stomach is flipping over and over … and then, before I've made a decision, Olivia returns.

"Can we go back to the park now?"

I can't leave this spot. Mum is there and I'm torn.

"Can we go back now?" repeats Olivia.

"Erm ... tell you what," I say, thinking on the spot. "Let's play a game."

"What game?" says Olivia.

"Erm … well … it's called being a Big Girl." It's the best I could come up with.

"We've already done that," says Olivia. "What about Batman?"

"Okay," I say, one eye on Mum, the other on Olivia. "Well how about, we have to save Gotham City from the Batcatcher?"

Mum finds a table and sits down.

"Who's the Batcatcher?"

"He's Batman's greatest enemy and he's after you."

"Nooo!" screams Olivia, giggling.

"And you need to get away quickly, while I create a diversion."

"What do you mean?"

"Well, you have to walk – nicely – to the park, all on your own … and when you get there, you have to wait at the swings, keep an eye out the baddies, and I'll be along in a minute." A minute. That's all I need. A minute to talk to Mum, to give her my number, to make plans…

Mum unwraps her food.

"Why? What are you going to do?"

I have to think quick. "I'm going to defeat the Batcatcher and when I do, I'll buy you the biggest ice cream you have ever seen!"

Olivia is won over.

I take her outside and press the button at the crossing. The green man is quicker this time, and I see Olivia safely back across the road. She skips off towards the park. I've got fingers crossed she won't do anything silly and I hope and pray I'm doing the right thing, but it's not as if I have a choice. Nobody in their right mind would pass up a chance to talk to the Mum they haven't seen for years.

I touch *My Mum's* bike. The fuel tank is still warm. *My Mum's* fuel tank.

And I pluck up the courage to go inside, walk past workmen in their overalls tucking into their breakfast burgers and hash browns, past teenagers, people probably on their way to work, or on a day off ... I don't care. The whole world could be in Maccy's and it wouldn't make any difference.

Butterflies turn somersaults in my stomach as I stand behind *My Mum*.

I can't help but smile.

But do I touch her on the shoulder?

Do I say hello?

Will she even recognise me after all this time?

And then ... and then (deep breath) I say it. "Mum?"

She turns round. "Elle!" She practically chokes on her coffee. "Don't do that again!"

"Sorry! Sorry." The last thing I wanted was to upset Mum and now I have, because she doesn't leap up and hug me or anything, and instead she wipes the coffee dribbles from her chin and checks her clothes. She takes a bite of her McMuffin and points to the seat next to her. I sit down.

I have a hundred questions to ask but opt for, "What are you doing here?"

She has a mouthful of food and doesn't answer.

"Did you see me on the internet?" I say. "Did you come to find me?"

Her answer: "I'm trying to eat here."

So I let her finish her mouthful and before she can get the next one in, I ask again. "So what are you doing here?"

She wipes her mouth with the back of her hand. "Well, I'm travelling now, Babe, with …" She stops talking to examine my face. "You're fatter than you used to be."

I hold my stomach in and straighten my back, trying to look thinner. "No, I don't think so," I say. "It's just been a long time, that's all."

Mum sighs. "Of course it has. Come here." And that's when she hugs me. The moment I have dreamed of for years.

I'm sitting next to Mum – *MY MUM* – with the biggest grin on my face, and nothing and no one can take it away. I am Margo, Edith and Agnes dancing with Gru. I am Dewey Finn, *'sticking it to the man'*. I am Phil telling Rita, *'Today is tomorrow. It happened, you're here.'*

"You okay, Babe?" says Mum.

And I nod, eagerly.

When Mum finishes her breakfast, she makes me stand up and do a twirl. "You need some decent clothes," she says. "Let's go shopping."

This is the end of my very own Groundhog Day and I couldn't be happier.

24.

I link my arm into Mum's and we march out of Maccy's, past her bike in the disabled parking bay and head for Star Buys. I glance up the road to check Olivia isn't hanging around, but she must already be at the park. It's been more than the promised minute and I know I should join her, but at the same time I cannot tear myself away from Mum. *Olivia will be fine. Olivia will be fine.*

In Star Buys Mum grabs some jeans and tops for me to try on and a handful of bras for herself. In the changing rooms, Mum strips off to the waist. I try not to look at her boobs but I'm sure they are bigger than they used to be. I stare at her tattoo instead – the ugly black skull where the Purple Emperor used to be is now a skull is now surrounded by red roses.

Mum sees me looking. "Isn't it gorgeous?"

It's horrible. "Yes, it's lovely."

Mum tries on a red lace bra. The red matches the roses. "Remember that *terrible* butterfly I used to have?" she says.

"The Purple Emperor," I say. "It wasn't terrible"

"No, it was," she says. "*Really* terrible. And it's because of that ridiculous thing I lost you."

That word – *lost* – makes it sound as if she was sad to *lose* me. "Did you miss me?" I ask.

Mum's looking at herself in the mirror. "Do you like it?" she says, wanting a second opinion on the bra instead of answering my question.

"Erm, yes. It's very nice."

"Aren't you going to try on those jeans?"

I nod, take off my shoes and trousers and grab a pair of the jeans.

Mum picks up a black, under-wired bra and says, "Which do you prefer, black or red?"

I hate them both. "I like them both," I say.

She picks up another bra – a white one – and gives it a quick once over but throws it down almost immediately. "No, not white," she says. "I'm not a fucking virgin. Lol."

"It's so lovely to see you," I say, pulling on the jeans.

"Yeah," she says, taking off the red bra and replacing it with the black one.

I look away and try to zip up the jeans. They're a skinny fit and way too tight for comfort. "What are you doing here, anyway?" I ask, again.

Mum turns from side to side, checking herself in the mirror.

"I mean … it's such a coincidence!" I say, wishing she'd join in the conversation so I have something to occupy my attention other than her boobs.

"Not really," she says. "I saw you on the web."

"So you *did* see me? With the butterfly?"

"Yep," she says, but she's back to the bra selection and picks up a purple one. It's pretty – my favourite colour – but she dismisses that too.

"You were looking for me?" I say. Of course she was looking for me. I'm her only daughter. Her only child. A day won't have passed when she wasn't looking for, or at least thinking about me, just as there hasn't been a day when I don't think about her.

Mum removes the black bra and hands it to me. "Kind of," she says.

"Kind of?"

"Well, I was actually looking for Billy," she says. "You remember Billy."

"Billy Slade?"

"Yeah, because I owe him…"

She owes Billy? What about me? "What do you owe him? He was horrible to you."

"Nooo … no he wasn't. He loved me."

"He dumped you for someone else after you got a tattoo to prove how much you loved him," I remind her.

"No, it wasn't like that. He was just trying to make a point that I wasn't his *only* option."

"He's in prison," I say.

"*Was* in prison. He's out now. And yeah, I did find him in case you were wondering … but that's when I found you in, so that's even better."

"You found me by accident?" I say. "By ACCIDENT?"

"A happy accident," she says.

I don't want to be an accident, even if it was a happy one.

"I'd been looking for Billy for weeks," she continues. "And out of desperation, put 'purple emperor' into the Google search bar. That's when I saw you. But then I bumped into Dan and he told me Billy was out of prison and gave me his address, so it all worked out after all."

We stop talking for a while and Mum tries on more clothes. She finds me some more jeans, which fit better, and a shirt, while she concentrates on bras. I'm not sure what to think or say. She found me by accident. So she wasn't looking for me?

"Did you miss me?" I ask again.

"Of course I missed you," she says.

"But you weren't looking for me … you were looking for Billy Slade." I can't let it go.

She stops admiring herself at last and turns to face me. "Oh Babe, you think I'd forgotten you, don't you?"

I shrug. It sounds silly. Of course a mother couldn't forget her daughter.

"Listen," she says. "If it makes you any happier, I've been trying to find you ever since … ever since the last time. But you moved, didn't you?"

"Several times," I say.

"Exactly."

"But you *have* been looking?"

"Sure, Babe. You're my kid, aren't you?"

I start to relax. It feels a little better, knowing I was right, knowing that Mum has always been looking for me, knowing she cares. "I tried looking for you too," I say.

"But you didn't find me, did you?" She laughs. "That's the beauty of the travelling life. You never stay in one place long enough for anyone to find you."

"I've been writing to you," I say.

"Where?"

"To that address you gave me. I even went there once, but no one had heard of you."

She laughs again. "I'm not surprised. I was only there a couple of weeks … Wait, you didn't send any more money did you?"

"No. Just the one lot."

"Phew! Scared me for a minute. I thought some bastard might have run off with it." And then, "Do you want those?" she says, pointing at the jeans.

"Erm... yes, please." I don't know how I'll explain them to Mo and Sid, but I'm not going to say no to Mum.

"Take them off then," says Mum. "What about the top? Do you want that too?"

"Okay. Thank you."

Mum waits while I take off the jeans and shirt and puts them back on the hangers. Mum takes them off the hangers, rips the labels out and searches for the security tags. She takes a magnet from her pocket and uses it to unlock the tags. She does the same with the black bra – whilst still wearing it – then puts her t-shirt and leather jacket on over the top. She stuffs her own, old bra, into her bag along with my new clothes, and zips it up.

"Don't look at me like that," she says. "You think I'm made of money?"

"Erm... no, sorry," I say. "It's just that I don't like..."

"Don't like what?" she snaps in a whisper.

"Don't like stealing?" I whisper back. I'm aware of my own hypocrisy.

"This isn't stealing," she says. "This is the redistribution of wealth. The pigs who own this place have got plenty of money. They won't miss the odd bra. In fact, they expect it. It's all calculated in their costs. So in a way, I'm doing them a favour."

I don't understand how that works, so don't say anything.

Mum gives me her bag. "Now you walk out ahead of me. Go on ... shoo! I'll see you over the road in five minutes."

I leave the changing room and walk through the shop, convinced everybody knows what I've been doing, conscious that I'm carrying the evidence in Mum's bag. What if someone stops me? What will happen? I don't like it and I'm tempted to just leave the bag and make a run for it. But what if it's got all Mum's valuables in there too and I go and lose them?

I take a deep breath and carry on walking.

Out of the shop. All okay.

Across the road. All okay.

I stand outside the chemist, watching the door, waiting for Mum. All okay.

And good as her word, five minutes later, Mum appears. She grabs her bag and starts off down the road.

I follow. "Where are we going?"

"The Wall of Death," she says, grabbing my hand tightly.

And it's not that I wouldn't follow her to the ends of the earth, but it's only in that moment I remember Olivia.

"OHMYGOD! OLIVIA!"

How could I? How could I? I hate myself.

"What are you on about?" says Mum.

I pull my hand free.

I completely forgot about Olivia. Mo and Sid will kill me.

"I've gotta go!" I say, and start running, leaving Mum – *My Mum,* the only Mum I've ever had, the mum I've longed to see for 8 years… And I don't even think about it till I'm half way to the park. Is Mum following? I don't have time to look round. I'll face the consequences when I've found Olivia.

I dodge past old ladies and mums with buggies.

Ignore the red man on the pedestrian crossing.

Nearly get hit by a car.

Squeeze through the park gate in front of kid on a scooter.

And make it to the play area in one piece. Out of breath – gasping for air – cursing my selfishness and stupidity...

But Olivia is not here!

My heart explodes and someone screams.

Me.

"OLIVIAAAA! OLIVIAAAA!"

Mum catches up with me. "Geez, Elle. What are you playing at?"

I explain about Olivia, inadequately. My words are a scramble of panic.

Mum puts her hands on my shoulders. "Slow down," she says. "We'll find the kid. Alright?" She's so calm. It helps, but I'm shitting myself.

Mum asks people in the playground. No one has seen Olivia. She starts walking and I follow. "Come on," she says. "She won't be far."

All I can think about is Olivia's lifeless little body sticking out from under a hedge and I don't know how I'll ever live with myself if she's hurt.

I'm scared.

Terrified.

Sid and Mo trusted me. Olivia was my responsibility. And now she's missing.

But Mum is cool.

"She'll be hiding," she says. "Kids are like that."

We walk – fast – around the park, eyes everywhere.

There's a bunch of lads playing football ahead, and my spirits lift. They're about Olivia's size. I pull Mum over to where they are and get her to ask the other mums and dads, all watching the game, if they've seen Olivia. They shake their heads, and look disapprovingly at Mum's leather jacket. I'm too worried to care.

"Where is she?" I cry. Literally. The tears start falling.

I am in so much trouble, but Olivia might be in even bigger trouble and it's my fault.

And that's when Mum says, "Does this Olivia kid like dressing up by any chance?"

I grab her arm. "Yes, Why?"

Mum points to the kiosk, where a small kid has covered herself in cardboard boxes of various shapes and sizes.

"OLIVIA!" I shout.

She turns round with a kind of jerky mechanical movement, and smiles.

I run over to her. "Olivia, why didn't you stay in the play area?" I say.

"I. Am. Batbot," she says in a robotic, monotone voice.

Mum joins us. "Hello, trouble," she says. They fist bump. It seems so natural between them. "Didn't your mum ever tell you not to go running off like that?" she says.

Olivia looks her straight in the eye and says, "My mummy's dead. We live with Mo and Sid and Green."

"She's my foster sister," I explain.

Mum yawns, looks at her phone and checks her messages

Olivia continues. "Mo bakes cakes and Sid is an actor, but Green is very very old and he reads the paper."

Mum looks up, suddenly interested. "So who's this Sid guy? What's he been in?"

"He's going to be Superdad," says Olivia. "On the telly."

"Is he now?" says Mum.

"And he's going to be very famous and very very rich," continues Olivia, confidently.

Mum nods approvingly. "Sounds like my kind of guy!"

"He hasn't actually got the job yet," I say. "And we should probably be getting home." I'm desperate to separate the two of them before the awkward questions start.

"Who are you, anyway?" says Olivia.

Too late.

But thanks to some minor miracle Mum's phone buzzes, and she doesn't answer Olivia. She reads her message and then tells me she has to go. "Sorry, Babe. People to meet. You know how it is."

She can't just go! "You can't just go," I say.

"No, but fancy getting together tomorrow?" she says.

I nod eagerly, grinning.

"Midday? On the sea front, by the mermaid? We can take in a show. Have a proper catch up then."

I have no idea how I'll do it, but I'll find a way. "Great!"

"Cool," says Mum. And then, "Laters, Babe."

I watch her run across the road, take out her phone and call someone. She doesn't look back. It's not the reunion I had always dreamed of. And now I have to answer a thousand questions from Olivia.

"Who was she?" says Olivia.

I shrug, as if I don't know. "Just some woman."

"What were you doing with her?"

"Looking for *you*," I say, accusingly.

"Why was she looking for me?"

"Because I couldn't find you on my own."

"Why are you seeing her again?"

"I'm not," I say.

"But you said you were."

"No I didn't."

"Yes you did."

"No I didn't."

"You did. I heard you."

"Oh that was just to shut her up."

"Why did you want to shut her up?"

"Just ... because ... you know ... she was kind enough to help me find you and I didn't want to be rude."

"Why is it rude?"

"Olivia! Please! Stop asking me bloody stupid questions!" I lose my temper. It's not her fault, but I just don't have the answers.

"You swore," she says.

"Yes, I'm sorry. I shouldn't have."

"Am *I* seeing her again?" she says.

"Who?"

"That lady." Like, she's not giving up that easily.

"No! Why would you do that?"

"Because she said she was going to see a show. Is it Mary Poppins?"

"Look, I have no idea. She was just some random weird woman," I say, firmly. "I felt sorry for her. She was lost too. But she helped me find you, so I didn't want to be rude. I'm not seeing her again, and neither are you. Okay?"

Olivia screws up her face and says, "But you said you would? That's lying."

I take a deep breath. "No, it's not lying. It's called sparing someone's feelings, okay?"

"No, if you don't tell the truth, it's lying."

"Okay, so it's what they call a good lie. Good lies are okay, because they come from the right place and mean well."

"What do bad lies do?"

"They upset people," I say. "We don't tell bad lies."

"What about half and half lies?"

"What? There's no such thing as half and half lies. I don't know what you mean."

"Well if there are good lies, and bad lies, there must be half and half lies. Like, I don't like nuts but I do like chocolate, so if I get a chocolate with a nut in it it's a half and half sweet..."

I grab Olivia's hand and start marching her towards Ocean Avenue. "Look, let's just forget this ever happened, eh? And if we do, I won't tell Mo and Sid you were a naughty girl and got lost."

"I wasn't lost! I knew where I was!"

"No, but you left the playground when I told you not to. So you were lost to me, okay? And that was VERY naughty."

Olivia looks down, shame-faced.

"So I won't tell on you, if you don't mention the woman to Mo and Sid, okay?"

Olivia nods.

"I mean it. We'll pretend this never happened, yes?"

"Okay."

After a while, Olivia says, "I didn't get my comic."

And I say, "No, because you were naughty."

"Or an ice cream."
"No, because you were naughty."
"But I'm hungry."
"Tough."
"Are you hungry?"
"No."
"And Green didn't get his newspaper. He's not naughty," she says.
"No, but I'll get it later…"
"What about my comic?"
And that's when I lose my temper. "No! Olivia, will you just SHUT UP!"
And finally she gets the message.

*

I have all my fingers crossed Olivia will keep quiet, but the actual second we walk through the door, Olivia says, "We met a woman in the park."

Mo looks at me, expecting illumination.

I pretend there isn't any, and shrug, as if I don't know what she's talking about.

"But we're not supposed to say anything," says Olivia.

Honestly? I want to hit her. Except that somehow I manage to restrain myself. "Olivia ran off," I say. "And a woman helped me find her. I'm really sorry. I didn't want to get her in trouble … and I didn't mean to lose her ... it's why we've been so long …"

But Mo is already distracted by Olivia rummaging through the kitchen cupboards, and Sid is way too busy going through his audition notes to worry about us. Neither of them gives me a hard time and I think I've got away with it.

25.

When I come down for breakfast, Sid is there packing, unpacking and repacking his bag, looking stressed. Doesn't help that Olivia is there too, tugging at his sleeve, asking question after question.

"What do you have to do? Where will you be? When will you be back? When will it start? What do you have to wear? What if you don't want to wear it? Will you miss us? Will you be famous? ..." On and on and on. She doesn't even wait for answers.

"Enough!" snaps Sid, finally. "I don't know, Olivia, but I'll tell you *everything* when I get back. I promise. Okay?"

Olivia runs off into the garden, close to tears.

Mo gives Sid a reproachful look, before following Olivia.

Sid sighs and shakes his head; grabs a lunchbox of sandwiches and stuffs them into his bag, and then pushes a folder across the table to me. "I stayed up last night trying to find things that might suit you," he said. "There's a selection in there. Have a look, see what you think. It's just a starting point."

The folder has 'Audition Prep' written on the front and inside there are several printed sheets of paper with poems on; another hand written piece with 'Possible Songs?' written at the top of the page. I smile and try to look pleased, but now Mum is back on the scene everything has changed. I don't know what my future holds but I doubt Weston will be a thing.

"Well? What do you think?" says Sid.

"Yeah, thanks. Looks .... umm great."

Sid nods and zips up his bulging bag. "Oh, and one more thing," he says, pulling a face with his words. "It's a big favour…"

A favour? People don't usually expect *favours* from me, unless they're Mum or Billy Slade asking me to be quiet, get out, or hide their stolen goods.

"… but I know I can trust you," he says, looking almost embarrassed. "It's just that Mo has a baking order she needs to get done and Olivia is going to be hard work without me here. You know what she's like. Would you mind stepping in and helping out? As much as you can ... I mean, we don't expect miracles ... just a little distraction. "

This is the last thing I need. "Can we watch movies?" I say.

"Do whatever it takes," says Sid. "And I'll make it up to you. Promise."

I agree, but it's not as if I have a choice.

*

We watch the van splutter out of the drive and down the road. Olivia is clearly trying not to cry, but as soon as the van is out of sight she runs inside. I follow her in. Her head is buried in a cushion and her body is racked with sobs, but when I tell her I've got a new game called Hunt the Hero. She looks up, interested. Mo thanks me silently and goes back to the kitchen.

"So how do you play it?" asks Olivia.

I tell her it's like hide and seek, except that I hide Olivia's Super Hero comics around the house and she has to find them. For every one that she finds, I promise to give her a magical superpower.

"Like what?"

"Like, invisibility ... or brains ... or ... the power to be kind!"

"Cool," says Olivia, falling for it and closes her eyes immediately.

I plant comics in the laundry basket, under beds and cushions, in cupboards and on shelves. And when I've finished I tell her to count to ten before she's allowed to look. She only reaches four, when we hear a thud in the hallway and Mo shouting. Olivia runs out of her bedroom and grabs my legs and I hold her hand and we run downstairs.

Green is lying on the floor, freakishly still. Mo is kneeling by his side shaking his shoulders, still shouting, "Dad? Can you hear me?"

"What's happening?" says Olivia.

"Call an ambulance," says Mo, to me.

I pick up the phone and dial 999. I give the woman at the other end all the information she asks for and she assures me an ambulance is on its way so I hang up.

Meanwhile, Olivia is freaking out. I hug her, stroke her hair, and tell her, "It's okay. It's okay. He'll be all right." I feel her body shaking.

Mo puts her head down in front of Green's face. "He's breathing," she says, at which point his whole body starts to twitch, and jerk, and then suddenly he's awake. "Dad? What happened?"

Green's reply is incoherent.

Mo tells him to lie still, that an ambulance is on the way, and everything will be all right. She asks me to fetch a blanket. So I run upstairs and pull the duvet from my bed. Olivia follows me like a shadow.

"I'm scared," she says.

"It's okay," I say. "Mo knows what to do." But I'm scared too.

We take the duvet downstairs and help Mo wrap it around Green. Olivia and I cling to each other until we hear a siren in the street. I open the front door and the ambulance crew rush into the house. Mo takes us to one side.

"Is he going to be all right?" asks Olivia.

"He's going to be fine," says Mo. (I don't believe her.) "But he's going to have to go to the hospital."

"Are you going with him?" I say.

"I can't leave you two," she says.

"You can," I say. "I'll look after Olivia. And Sid will phone home when he stops, won't he? I'll ask him to come home." It's an instinctive response. I don't think it through.

Mo bites her lip. You can tell she is torn. "I'll text him. Tell him to call you. Just to be sure."

The paramedics, meanwhile, have lifted Green into a kind of wheelchair trolley thing and they talk to him while fitting various gismos and wires to his arm and chest. He's got a breathing mask on too. His arms have stopped twitching and jerking.

We watch them wheel him out to the ambulance.

"Go," I say to Mo.

"I'd better just call Sasha," says Mo.

"No, don't worry. I'll do it. And I'll stay with Olivia. We'll be all right. I promise." I turn to Olivia. "Won't we?"

Olivia nods, uncertainly, so I put my arm around her to reassure and she holds my hand.

Mo looks from the ambulance to me, to Olivia, and back to her dad.

"Please go," I say. "Green needs you there."

And Mo says, "If you're sure?"

I nod.

We watch the ambulance drive away, blue light flashing.

I try to carry on as if nothing has happened; hiding comics and making superpower promises to Olivia I can't keep – invisibility, the strength of The Hulk, flight, enemy zappers and so on. When I run out of ideas I turn to bribery, raiding the kitchen cupboards and offering her cooking chocolate, hundreds and thousands and glitter sprinkles to eat. We play sleeping lions, except that when she is not 1000% occupied Olivia can't stop her tears.

I wish Sid would phone. The later he leaves it, the less likely it will be that he's back in time for me to meet Mum, and if I call Sasha it will be impossible to get away, but I CANNOT not see Mum.

I put *Despicable Me* on the TV. Olivia liked it before, but it's not helping today and her tears are starting to frustrate and annoy me. I get the cooking chocolate out again. At least if she's eating, she won't be crying, except that there is not enough cooking chocolate in the world to satisfy Olivia and when we run out it's tears again. I suggest washing up, pull a chair in front of the sink and tie Mo's big apron around Olivia's middle. She turns on the tap, empties practically the whole bottle of washing up liquid into the sink and is at least distracted by the bubble mayhem long enough for me to collect pots and pans and mugs, and line them up for Olivia to wash, and finally, the phone rings.

It's Sid. He sounds angry. "Let me speak to Mo," he says.

"She's not here... Didn't you get her text?"

"No. Where is she? I need to talk to her..." He doesn't let me get a word in edgeways. "The van's broken down! I'm stuck on a slip road and going to miss the audition..."

I tell him about Green and the ambulance.

Sid is horrified. "So, it's just you two? On your own?"

"Yes, but we're okay. Can you come home? How long will you be?" I glance at the clock.

He groans and moans and makes all kinds of noises I can't understand.

"What?" I say.

"I'm stuck, Elle. I don't know. This is a nightmare..."

Stuck? "What, you're not going to get home?" I say.

"I can't, Elle. I'm waiting for someone to tow the van."

Panic is already rising in my chest. What if Mum turns up and I'm not there? What if she thinks I don't care? What if I never see her again?

"I'll call Sasha," says Sid.

"I've already tried," I lie, a despicable plan already forming in my head, which won't work if Sasha is here. "She's busy, but listen, we're all right. We're playing games. Having fun. And I'm old enough to look after Olivia for a few hours. You just sort out the van, and I'll wait here with Olivia."

Sid only agrees because he has no choice.

*

"This is the plan," I tell Olivia. "I need to go out..."

"Why?"

"Because you've been a very good girl and you deserve a surprise!"

Olivia smiles, pleased with herself. "What is it?"

"If I tell you it won't be a surprise."

"Why do we need to go out?"

"No, *I* need to go out, and you have to stay here..."

"On my own?" she says. Her little face drops. I am the worst person in the world, but I can't back out now.

"You'll be fine," I say, trying to jolly her along. "Just don't answer the phone, or the door – not to ANYONE – do you understand?"

"Why can't I come?" she says.

I can't think of an answer and Olivia doesn't look happy. I'm not surprised. I'm doing a terrible thing, leaving her, especially after nearly losing her yesterday, but what choice do I have?

"Why can't I come?" she says, again.

"Because it will ruin the surprise."

"Suppose I don't want a surprise?" she says.

"Suppose I got you two surprises?" I say.

She thinks about it. "Three?" she says.

I take a deep breath, as if I've got to really think about it, but you know what? Lying just gets easier and easier. "Okay, Olivia. If you're *very very very* good, I'll get you three surprises. Okay?"

"How will you know if I'm good when you're not here?" she says. Kid logic.

"Because I've got special eyes that can see places where I'm not."

"Like a super hero?" she says.

"Exactly," I say.

I make her a sandwich and put a couple of Mo's cakes on a plate and cover them in cling film. I make sure she has plenty to drink too. Then I lock all the doors and windows, tell her a whole list of things she's allowed and not allowed to do, drag out my old mobile phone and write the number on a piece of paper so Olivia can call me if she really needs me.

And then I – Elle Mackenzie, the 16 year-old wicked heartless daughter of a bank robber – leave a five year-old wannabe superhero all alone.

26.

I see Mum before she sees me. She's near the mermaid statue, as promised, which is next to a kind of giant topless structure with HARLEY'S WALL OF DEATH written large across the side. There are dozens of hairy bikers milling around and Mum appears to be deep in conversation with one of them. My heart sinks a little. I wanted us to be alone together.

When Mum sees me, she waves.

The man turns round. It's Billy Slade.

I nearly run back to Ocean Avenue, except I've waited too long for this.

"You've grown," says Billy, eyeing me up and down. "Long time, no see, eh?" He laughs. His teeth have turned black, his hair is falling out and he looks terrible. I hope he doesn't know it was me who told the police about the robbery.

Mum and Billy continue their conversation and barely acknowledge my presence. I feel like a spare part, shuffling awkwardly on the spot, trying to look interested in the Wall of Death. I notice a new tattoo on Billy's neck – flames, reaching up around the back of his head. It looks weird – not just because it looks as if his head is resting on a bed of fire, but because a tatty beard has grown over some of the tattoo and spoils the effect. I try not to stare.

It suddenly dawns on me that when Mum said we'd go to a show, this is the show she meant. Not exactly Mary Poppins.

Eventually, Billy Slade wanders off and Mum turns to me. "You're late," she says.

"Sorry," I say. "Something happened at home."

She doesn't ask what. "Have you got any cash?"

"No, sorry. I didn't think I'd need any."

She harrumphs, checks her wallet, says, "Okay, I've got just enough, but I can't afford merch so don't bother asking."

"I don't want merch," I say eager to please. "And anyway, I can't stay long because..."

Because nothing. Mum isn't listening.

She shoves a Tesco carrier bag into my arms and says, "You left these behind," and then pushes me through the crowd. We reach the ticket office seconds after the shutter slams down. Mum bangs on the metal.

A gruff old man voice on the other side, shouts, "Full. Next show in three hours."

Mum won't take no for an answer. She bangs again.

I peer into the Tesco carrier and see the clothes we stole from Star Buys.

Meanwhile, Mum shouts and swears at the metal shutter about how she has come miles for this and demands to be let in. A couple of leather clad bikers nearby, egg her on, jeering and whistling, but the shutter doesn't open again. We hear the rev of bike engines inside, and the crowd cheering.

Mum turns to me. "Why didn't you get here earlier?" she's angry.

"I'm sorry," I say. "There was a problem at home ..."

She doesn't listen; just marches off and I have no choice but to follow.

We stop at a burger van which smells of bacon. Mum orders two black coffees, hands one to me and sits on a wooden bench overlooking the beach.

I sit down too.

"I really wanted to see that," she says, sulking like a little kid.

"I'm sorry, but I couldn't get away."

"We'll have to go to the next show," she says.

I feel a weight in my stomach. The weight of letting her down. "I can't," I say. "I need to be home for Olivia…"

She raises her eyebrows and swears again.

I feel bad – even though I shouldn't – and wonder why everything in my life always goes wrong. I look down at my unwanted drink and my Tesco carrier full of stolen clothes, wondering how I will explain them to Mo and Sid. We listen to the sound of the bikes roaring and the crowd cheering. I count the bikes all parked up in a row for as far as the eye can see – twenty four before I lose interest – and feel my leg touching Mum's leg before she jerks it away and throws her empty coffee cup on the floor.

I put my undrunk coffee under the bench when Mum isn't looking.

"So what are you running home for?" she says, eventually. There's contempt in her voice.

I hesitate, but tell her anyway. "Well, the old guy who lives with us, Green, he's in hospital."

"Is he gonna die?" says Mum.

"No! I mean, I hope not."

Mum rolls her eyes. "Then what's the big deal?"

I explain about Green and Mo being at the hospital and Sid going for his audition.

Mum yawns. "So what's the problem?"

"So I'm supposed to be looking after Olivia," I say.

"The kid?"

"And she'll be wondering where I am."

"She'll be fine," says Mum, dismissively. "Borrow my phone if you like. Tell her to behave."

If only it were that simple. "No, I'd best go home. I just wanted you to know that I wasn't standing you up and wondered if we could meet tomorrow instead."

Mum shakes her head. "I dunno, Babe. Depends." She doesn't say on what, and starts picking up bits of gravel and stones to hurl at the gulls. They squawk and fly away, then come back for leftover junk food littering the path. After a while, Mum says, "So how long have you been with this family?"

"A couple of months," I say.

"Do you like them?"

I nod. "Yes. They're nice.

"And they like you?"

"Yes," I say. Finally, Mum is taking an interest.

"So how come you've moved about so much? Are *you* the problem? Or is it *them?*"

I'd like to blame everyone else, but I can't. I shrug. "I haven't been exactly well behaved," I say. I look down at my feet, feeling embarrassed.

Mum laughs. "Like mother like daughter, eh?" She continues to throw stones at the seagulls. "Just don't let them dump you in one of them hostels," she says. "Because they're bad news. You'll hate it."

"How do you know?"

She hits a seagull. "Got it!"

We watch it limp away.

"How do you know about hostels?" I ask.

"You don't want to know," she says, taking aim again.

"No, but I do," I say. "I want to know everything. Because … well, it's been a long time and we've got a lot of catching up to do."

Mum shakes her head. "Geez Elle, you pick your moments don't you?"

I shrug, bite my lip, apologise. I shouldn't be so nosey.

But after a while, Mum says, "Okay. I'm sorry. You've got a right to know. After all, I'm the reason you're in care. If my own life had been happier, perhaps I'd have been a better mother... Perhaps you'd understand why I've done the things I've done. So I'll tell you. I'll tell you everything. The story of my life, by Stevie Mackenzie, aged thirty four and a half."

I laugh, and for the first time in six years, feel as if we might be having a moment; a mother/daughter moment – a moment I'll want to treasure – and she goes on to tell me the stuff about her life I never knew. She was born in Southend on Sea and taken into care when she was two. Apparently her mum used to go out 'on the rob' (as she put it) and leave her alone in the flat.

She stops then and looks me in the eye. "I never left you alone that young, in case you're wondering."

"No, no, of course not," I say, not entirely convinced.

Mum moved from foster home to foster home and ended up in a residential school in Wigan. She never saw her mum again. "Out of sight, out of mind," she says. "And she's probably dead by now anyway."

I feel sad and sorry for her, but try not to show it because Mum is talking like it's all water off a duck's back, like she doesn't really care.

"They put me in a hostel eventually," she says. "A transition hostel they called it. Fucking dreadful place; full of the living dead. The worst place they ever dumped me – and that's saying something. Long story short, they kicked me out when I was sixteen, and pregnant …"

"With me?"

"No, a boy. Had to give him up for adoption."

"I've got a brother?" I cry, suddenly filled with a hundred questions. "What's he look like? Do you know his Dad? Why didn't you keep him? Where is he now? What's his name? …"

"Babe!" she cries, holding up her hands. "Enough!"

I bite my lip.

"Let's not talk about him. This is about me and you."

But I'm in shock. Not only has Mum's life has been more like mine than I ever imagined, I have a brother. I have a brother? Yes, that's what she said. I have a brother.

"So then you came along" she continues without any explanation. "And we got put in a mother's hostel..."

I have a brother.

"...Which was better than the other one but everyone had a kid, and day or night there was always someone crying – and I'm not just talking about babies..."

I have a brother.

"...Until finally, the council found me a flat and things started to improve..."

But I can't let it pass. "Do you know where my brother is?"

She stops talking for a second, looks at me as if I'm mad. "I said, enough. I dunno where he is. He could be anywhere. They don't tell you stuff like that."

I ask if she's ever tried to find him, but she shakes her head and rambles on about ex boyfriends, her favourite take-aways and how she can't resist a man in leather, but I've zoned out. The life story of Stevie Mackenzie, aged thirty four and a half, is more like a catalogue of her failures as a mother.

But then she says, "... But you were such a cute kid. Do you remember how we used to cut faces out of toast? And spray paint the walls at the back of the town hall before they chased us away? Do you remember joining that little music group in the church? You learned to play the tambourine and you could sing too; every one said you were really good..."

"You never told me that before."

"S'pose I thought you'd remember."

"No, I mean, you never told me I was a good singer."

"Didn't want you getting big-headed, did I? But I should have got you in a band ... Yeah, babe, we could have been rich by now."

"It's not all about money, though, is it?"

"Debateable," laughs Mum. "Cos you can't do anything without it ... that's why Billy Slade was so good for me ... sorry, *IS* so good for me." She has a faraway look in her eye and a smile on her face, both of which I resent. "And yeah, I know he's not God's gift in the looks department, but he's got a good heart..."

No, he hasn't.

"... And he didn't deserve to be banged up. If it wasn't for that bag of cash he chucked me I'd have been destitute. If I ever find out who ratted on him, I'll kill him."

My cheeks flush. I look away from Mum so she can't see the tell-tale signs of guilt.

She picks up another stone and aims it at a huge gull on top of a bollard. She misses. The bird circles overhead before flying away. Mum laughs. "Anyway, happy now?" as if that's it, everything I need to know to understand how we ended up here, locked out of the Wall of Death on Cockle Bay seafront, throwing stones at gulls.

"I never knew all that," I say.

"Yeah, well you're not the only one who's had it hard."

I feel sorry for Mum. And angry too. I want to hold her hand or give her a hug and make all the bad stuff disappear so we can just be happy, but I'd rather she hugged me and made my bad stuff disappear, or at least asked for my life story, because that's what mums are supposed to do, right? When she doesn't, I pick up a handful of stones and throw them, one by one, at a crushed beer can blowing along the path. I hit it three out of five times.

When Mum has a go, she hits it every time, and brags, "Beat you, kid!"

Is this how it it's always going to be, I wonder? Maybe I shouldn't have come here after all. Maybe I should be home with Olivia, in Ocean Avenue, worrying about Green, and planning my future with the Love family.

And then Mum says something which takes me by surprise. "So anyway, I've been thinking about our future together..."

"Our future?" I say. "Yours and mine?"

"Obviously," says Mum.

"Together?"

"Why do you think I asked you to meet me today?"

I have to check again. "You want me to live with you?"

She shrugs. "Why not?" she says.

Without even thinking I fling my arms around her. This must be what winning the lottery feels like. She doesn't even push me away.

"I want it to be like old times, Babe," she says. "You and me and Billy."

My euphoria balloon bursts.

I let go of her. "Billy Slade?"

"Sure. We're planning a new start, together, with you."

I don't want a new start with Billy. He was the reason we stopped being happy in the first place. He was the reason we were forced apart...

"What do you say? Fancy it? 'Cause it'll be just perfect, won't it?"

And then Sasha's voice pops up in my head. *Given that your mother is still wanted in connection with a bank robbery, living with her is not likely to be a scenario we have to consider.* There's no way I'm going to be allowed to run off into the sunset and live happily ever after with Mum and Billy Slade.

"They'll never let me, Mum."

"Obviously, Babe! We're not exactly the model family, are we?"

"So what are you thinking? Where will we live? How will it work?"

"We're going to Australia."

"Australia?" Surely not again...

She sees my doubt. "This isn't like last time, Babe. It's all planned. It's really gonna happen."

"But how will we get there? I mean, if you're still wanted for the robbery and I'm *running away*..." air quotes, "won't they stop us? I don't have a passport or anything."

"Ah but Billy knows someone. Dave. He deals in visas and passports. It'll cost a bit, but once we've got the cash, we'll buy our way out of here."

"But visas take weeks or months to come through," I say, remembering Green's words.

"Who told you that? Because it's rubbish. Dave gets them all the time. He sorts everything. And then it'll be just you, me and Billy, lying on Bondi Beach, having tea with kangaroos, throwing steaks on a barbie. Doesn't that make you excited?"

An aeroplane flies above us, leaving a white scar in the blue sky. We both watch it pass. I'm not as excited as I thought I would be. It's too much like the last time.

And then I say, "How long will it take to get everything sorted?"

Mum draws breath through her teeth. "That's the tricky bit. Dave won't do anything without cash up front. Once he's got the money, it should take ... oooh, a week tops, maybe only a couple of days." She starts to count silently on her fingers, as if she's adding things up, working things out. "So, I'm selling the Harley – which is a couple of grand at least – and Billy's got some knock-off stuff he can flog... " She pulls a pained expression. "But we'll still be short a few hundred. What do you think?"

Is she asking me to help? Because the Loves don't have cash lying around; they don't have a closed shop and full cash register overnight. And even if they did, I don't want a repeat of the past. I want Mum to find the cash, to commit to being with me, to prove her love. "So where will you get it from?" I say.

She weighs up some options in her head and says, "Honestly, Babe? I don't know yet, but I'm working on it. Trust me. We're family, after all. And family stick together."

It's that word – family – that gets me. "And … my brother?" I dare to say.

"Your brother?"

"The baby you gave up for adoption?"

"What about him?" Mum looks angry. Maybe she doesn't want to be reminded, but I've started so I have to finish.

"Well … he's family too … isn't he?"

Mum raises an eyebrow, stares at me and then breathes a big exasperated sigh before saying, "Okay, if it makes you happy, we'll try and find him."

I smile and thank her, wondering what my brother would be like. Older than me but maybe we look alike? Maybe he likes films too? Maybe we have other things in common? I've seen TV programmes where people are reunited with long lost family and it always seems to go so well. And now it's my own long lost family, about to be reunited… I cannot help but feel excited, happy, and contented; feeling as if everything will work out.

But as a kid carrying a helium balloon skips past us, followed by his mum and dad, I remember Olivia.

OH MY GOD I'VE DONE IT AGAIN!

What was I thinking?

What kind of a sister am I, anyway? "Mum," I say. "I'm going to have to go. Olivia's home alone. I'm really sorry ..."

WHAT WAS I THINKING?

Mum doesn't argue. She writes a number on a scrap of paper and hands it to me. "That's my mobile. Call me," she says. "And we'll meet back here in a couple of days."

"When, exactly?"

"Call me, and we'll fix something, all right?"

I nod, wishing it wasn't all so vague. Mum sees the look on my face. "But I'm not going to disappear off the face of the earth again ... I promise." She understands.

Reassured, I take the number and hold it close to my heart. "Thanks," I say. I move to hug her and she hugs back.

I run all the way back to Ocean Avenue, slightly in credit with the Bank of Hope. Except that when I get home, my worst nightmare is realised.

"Where have you been?" says Sasha.

"Just popped out," I say. "I wasn't long."

"I've been here for two hours," she says. "Sid rang to tell me about his situation. He told me you'd already rung but that I was, *busy,* which is another lie, isn't it? So I thought I'd better pop round, to check ... to see if I could be of any help."

I look at the ground, embarrassed.

"So where were you?" she says.

I look at Olivia, I see her eyes are red from crying and she has something sticky in her hair. I feel bad.

"Well?"

I shrug. "Out?"

"Obviously. Where?"

"Just out."

She looks at the Tesco carrier bag. "What's in there?"

"Oh … erm … I found it … I was, erm, going to hand it in at the police station."

Sasha raises an eyebrow. "Were you? How very public spirited of you, Elle," she says, sarcastically. "Give it to me and I'll do it."

I hand over the bag. Sasha looks inside, raises her eyebrows then tucks it into her social worker's satchel. I try to try to change the subject, hoping this will all go away. "Cup of tea?" I ask.

"I'm not here for cups of tea," she says, scornfully.

"What about you, Olivia? Do you want something to eat?"

She blows a raspberry and asks me where her surprises are.

I pull the kind of face which says, *you don't deserve a surprise because you cried* – and I feel like a terrible person. But attack is my only defence.

In the kitchen, I'm met with total devastation. The kitchen has been trashed good and proper. From top to bottom, there are cakes and biscuits everywhere, flour and sugar and jars of honey and jam tipped all over the floor, eggs splattered on walls, and cupboard doors left open with all their contents pulled out. The piece of paper with my telephone number on is coated with jam and stuck to the sink. My Audition Prep folder and all its contents have been torn into a hundred million pieces and scattered, like confetti over everything else.

"Holy Batman!" I say.

When I turn round, Sasha is standing in the doorway, checking my reaction.

"Olivia?" I say.

"Obviously," she says. "She thought you were dead! You selfish, selfish girl. And clearly I'm going to have to report this ... but I wouldn't be surprised if *both* of you end up in residential care. You're both out of control and Mo and Sid can't handle either of you."

I want to argue with her, but there isn't any point.

By the time Sid arrives home, I've made a start on the kitchen. Because yes, I feel bad about it happening in the first place, but also because it gets me out of Sasha's eyeline, who seems intent on writing reports and making phone calls.

Olivia meanwhile is acting like the Little Miss Perfect, sitting quietly next to Sasha, good as gold, watching crap TV and sucking her thumb.

The van was been towed to a nearby garage.

Sid apologises profusely; says the circumstances were *exceptional* and that I must have had *a good reason* to go out. He's really sorry. It won't ever happen again. He'll talk to me; get to the bottom of it ... but please could she come back when Mo is there? He's practically on his knees, begging for forgiveness.

Sasha's response is cold and business-like. She has to *speak to people*. "You'll hear from me tomorrow," she says as she is leaving.

After Sasha has gone, Sid won't talk to me. Doesn't ask me where I was, or what I thought I was doing, and he certainly doesn't try to get to the bottom of it. For once, he is all pinched lips and silent fury, but only with me. He's all over Olivia, promising her the earth to make up for "the NEGLECT". He spits out that last word, and it lands firmly in the pit of my filthy guilty soul.

He speaks to Mo on the phone.

I hear him telling her about Sasha and that she's coming back tomorrow. He wouldn't be surprised if they put us *'somewhere else'* (and, no, he *'isn't going to go into it on the phone in front of the kids.'*) Then he tells Mo about the van and how much it will cost to repair – more if they want it back quickly. He says they don't have the money and they'll have to let it go. He's quiet while Mo replies. And then loudly, he says, "But that's our savings!"

I shouldn't be listening, but I can't help myself.

Sid comes off the phone. Tells us to put on our shoes.

"Are we going to the hospital to see Green?" I ask.

Sid doesn't answer. Just marches us down the road as far as the post office. There's a cashpoint outside and he puts his card in, presses some buttons and stops. He stares at the screen for ages, and then punches the wall and swears. His card reappears, followed by a little white slip of paper which he screws up and throws in the gutter. He pulls another card from his pocket and feeds it into the machine, goes through the same button pressing routine and seconds later that card also reappears. This time it's followed by money. He repeats the whole operation, counts the two lots of twenty pound notes and puts them in his pocket, before marching us home.

Back in the house, Sid puts the money in the bureau.

I browse through the shelf of DVDs.

The only words Sid speaks to me, are, "You should watch Home Alone."

*

When Mo returns, the atmosphere is a vacuum; joy has been sucked out of the house leaving only long faces and serious smiles. I ask how Green is.

"He's in the right place," says Mo.

I don't ask what that means.

The kitchen is still a mess, but better than it was. Dinner – pasta with cheese – is made, and eaten, in silence. I notice the glossy HOME from HOME leaflets on the side, now stained with jam residue, and when everyone has finished eating I pick up the leaflets and flick through them, trying to provoke some reaction.

Sid looks away, but Mo bites. "I'm sorry Elle. Our hands are tied and we have to consider the possibility of you moving on." Her voice is controlled and her face is like stone. It's all very matter-of-fact, as if the last couple of months have meant nothing.

I nod – hurt – like I understand. And I do, I do. I just wish it could all be different.

"It's not what we want," she adds. "And I mean that. We really don't want to lose you. We've loved having you here." Loved – past tense. "You do know that, don't you?"

"Yes," I say. Except I wouldn't blame them if they were happy to see the back of me.

Mo offers ice cream for pudding. There are no cakes left. I don't want to eat anyway.

Olivia isn't hungry either. "Can we play Batman, instead?" she says to Sid. She's already wearing her curtain cape and eye mask.

Sid gets up wearily to take Olivia out to the garden. He half smiles at me when he leaves – not a real smile – and it's like he's trying to pretend he still cares about me when obviously he doesn't. How could he? I've signed my own leaving card. I've ruined everything. And if I do end up in HOME from HOME, I will only have myself to blame.

I help Mo restore the kitchen to how it used to be. There's an awful lot of wasted food in the bin and the cupboards are empty. Mo calls Miriam and tells her she won't be able to bake for a few days but she doesn't explain why. I'm grateful to her for that.

"How's Green?" I ask, desperate for a change of subject.

"He's not well," says Mo. "Not well at all."

And then, after more unnatural silence, I say, "Sorry."

Mo finally softens. "Oh Elle, where were you?" she says. "What did you think you were playing at?"

I want to tell Mo about Mum, I really do, and I think she'd understand because if anyone will, she will. But there's an expression I've heard people use – *between a rock and a hard place* – and that's where I am right now. If I don't tell the truth, Mo will think I'm a bad person. If I do tell the truth, she'll have to tell Sasha and Sasha will have to tell the police and Mum will be arrested.

Mo holds my hand and looks into my eyes. She's waiting for an answer.

"Look, I ... I needed some time on my own," I say. "That's all. Because Olivia was really getting on my nerves. I'm sorry. And I know I messed up ... but Olivia is okay, isn't she? Nothing terrible happened ..." Even as I'm saying it, I know it's wrong. Something terrible DID happen. Olivia was scared and trashed the kitchen and cried. And Sasha turned up and now they want to send me away, and possibly Olivia too.

Mo stiffens again. She knows it's a lie. "I thought we'd moved on," says Mo. "I thought you had turned a corner."

And those words – those carefully chosen words – gift-wrapped in accusation and disappointment, sting like nothing else ever stung before. I've let Mo down, and I've let Sid down and I've blown the best placement I ever had.

I take myself off to bed early. I need to be on my own and try to sleep; hoping that when I wake up everything will feel better. But I can't shake the waking nightmare ahead of me. There's a forked path. One road leads to HOME from HOME, a transition hostel full of the living dead. The other road leads to Australia, golden beaches and Mum. But to get there, we have to go via Dodgy Dave and Billy Slade and some serious fund raising. Both roads are strewn with ruts and potholes and I don't know how to navigate my way around them. I turn over and bury my head in the pillow, trying to pretend I'm not the world's biggest loser, trying to pretend I haven't just blown my last chance of happiness, trying not to hate myself. When I can't pretend, I throw back the covers, sit on the edge of my bed and wrestle with panic...

What do I do?

The van money calls my name.

But no. I can't take that. It wouldn't be fair.

Life isn't fair.

And that money – Sid's savings – are just sitting in the bureau, doing nothing.

And the van isn't even ready yet so no one would notice it gone for ages.

But Sid and Mo have been so good to me.

Except that if I have to go to HOME from HOME that won't matter.

And Mum and I could be together...

I climb out of bed, pull the turquoise suitcase from under the bed and throw all my worldly possessions inside. I find Mum's number, pull on my jeans, trainers and silky jacket and creep downstairs to the bureau. The money is still there. Even after everything they know about me, Mo and Sid are pushovers. I count five hundred pounds and put it down again.

Can I really do this?

Can I steal from Mo and Sid?

Could I live with myself if I do?

Could I live in HOME from HOME if I don't?

I pick up the money, count out four hundred pounds, put the rest back and close the bureau.

I'm almost out of the door when I change my mind.The extra hundred pounds could make a difference.

Finally, I pick up my phone and let myself out of the house. It's been a long time since I last ran away, and I'd forgotten how good it feels – as if there's a warm light at the end of a long cold tunnel, as if I'm in charge of my own life, as if I'm free ... at last.

27.

"Elle? What the fuck?" says Mum. "It's the middle of the night."

"I know, but you said to call if I had news. And I've got some. I've got money. Five hundred pounds. Is it enough?"

Silence.

"Mum? Can you hear me? I've got the money."

"Are you messing about?"

"No, seriously. Five hundred pounds."

"Really? You've got it?"

I hear a man's voice – Billy Slade – and then Mum whispering, "It's Elle. She's got cash…"

"Mum?" I say.

"Yes, Baby. I'm here. That's amazing. Where are you? I'll come now."

Mum and I arrange to meet at the end of the road. I don't want her rocking up on the Harley and waking the neighbourhood. It's just as well Green isn't here to hear it because he'd pick out that sound in the middle of a million other noisy sounds and be there, with his pen, writing down the number plate. The thought of Green makes me smile. I hope he's home soon, even if I won't be here. I think about how we turned a corner, how I helped him to see the butterfly and how he seemed happier afterwards. He's the closest thing to a granddad I'll ever have … yes, I hope he'll be home soon.

Mum takes ages to arrive.

A shed load of 'what ifs' rain down on me. What if she's had an accident? What if she's been stopped by the police? What if they recognise her for the robbery? What if she's arrested? What if she's changed her mind? What if she doesn't show? What if I end up in HOME from HOME? And then I hear it. The cough and splutter of her Harley, coming round the corner. Her beam shines right in my face and I have to shield my eyes. When the bike stops in front of me, the light goes off and I see Billy Slade.

"Have you got the money?" he says.

I nod. "Where's Mum?" I say.

"She's getting everything ready."

"Ready?"

"Erm ... yeah, for Australia?" he says, making it sound like a question.

"But I thought she needed the money first ... to give to Dave."

"Yeah, that's right, but she's erm ... she's with him now, and she sent me to get the cash so we could tie this up quickly."

I pull the envelope containing Sid's van money out of my jeans pocket. I don't know why because I definitely don't want Billy Slade anywhere near it.

But he grabs it, opens the envelope and counts the cash.

He smiles and says, "Well done. Stevie will be very pleased with this." He looks at my suitcase. "What's that?"

"My clothes and stuff," I say.

"Why?"

"Doh! Because I'm coming with you, obviously."

Billy Slade laughs. "Yyou've got that wrong," he says. "Think about it. If you go missing in the middle of the night, every police force in the country will be out looking for you. You're going to have to play the long game, wait for the visa and passports to arrive …. Wait for us to come and get you, and then … then we'll make a quick getaway. Understand?"

"Oh … yes, I didn't think of that," I say, feeling both stupid and sick, because this is almost definitely a repeat of what happened before.

"You don't think enough, that's your trouble," says Billy Slade, climbing back on the Harley.

"Wait," I say.

"What?"

"How long will it take?" I say.

"How long's a piece of string?"

"But how will l know it's time?" I say.

And he says, "We'll meet you tomorrow for an update. Same time, same place? Think you can manage that?"

He starts the engine.

I feel sick because I know I'll never see that money again.

But as he speeds away down the road, I make a mental note of the number plate: QZY 123

28.

It's late when I finally wake up. I check my face in the mirror. There are bags under my eyes from not enough sleep, an overdose of regret and more what ifs.

Mo's in the hallway talking to someone on the phone, agitated, angry. "Now is not a good time ... We're trying to keep spirits up here. ... Tell me this isn't true ... I don't care how good it is, she needs stability ... You can't move her every time there's a problem…"

She's obviously talking to Sasha. About me. I feel guilty for causing so much grief. If only I could tell everyone I'd be out of their hair any day now and all this angst and upset will be over, because yes, I've taken a huge overdraft at the Bank of Hope. But the best I can do now is to hide in the kitchen and make toast.

"You've done what?" continues Mo. "Without even consulting us?"

I can't listen anymore and close the kitchen door. I put bread in the toaster, grab myself a plate, a knife and some peanut butter and try to act normal.

Mo comes through and puts the kettle on. "I suppose you heard all that?" she says.

"I'm not going to that place," I say.

"Sasha wants you to have a look, that's all. She thinks you'll like it. And she's agreed to let me go with you."

I don't believe it's just *a look*. Once I'm through the doors they'll keep me there. "I'm not going," I say. "I don't want to live in a *hostel*. I'm sorry about leaving

Olivia – and I am, *really* sorry – but apart from that I haven't done anything wrong. I've been good since I've lived here haven't I? You know I have ..." My toast pops up. I spread it with peanut butter and wonder why I am such a hypocrite, because *good* has never been an adjective I've been blessed with.

"It would help if you told us what you were doing when you left Olivia, because I know there must have been a good reason." She smiles, and adds, "Because everyone makes mistakes, but we have to find a way to move on."

I am moving on; I'm moving to Australia.

"Tell the truth, Elle," says Mo. "It's the only way."

But it's not. There is another way and any day now, I'll be gone. Fingers crossed.

I am moving on; I'm moving to Australia.

I bite into my toast. The back door bursts open. Olivia runs inside, covered in mud. Sid follows, also covered in mud but not as bad as Olivia. I can't imagine what they've been doing, but they're giggling and laughing and mucky hands are everywhere.

Mo suddenly loses it. "Stop!" she cries. "We're in the middle of something here."

Sid looks from Mo to me, and back to Mo. "Oops. Sorry," he says. And then, "Come on, Olivia. We need to run you a bath." He takes Olivia's hand and they move towards the door.

"Wait!" I cry, surprising both myself and everyone else. "I want to apologise to Olivia"

Olivia and Sid let go of each other's hands and Olivia looks at me.

"Olivia," I say. "I'm really sorry I left you on your own. And I'm really sorry you got so upset." I feel nods of approval from Sid and Mo, but I can't look at them. They're probably waiting for the explanation I'm not going to give. It's enough to have said sorry. Olivia obviously agrees because she comes over to me, wraps her arms around my middle, and says, "Will you give me a bath?"

I look at Mo, to see if that's allowed.

She sighs and shakes her head, but gives in. Our *discussion* was over, anyway.

Upstairs, I run the bath water while Olivia gathers all her plastic animals. We tip bubble bath into the water, followed by the animals, and finally Olivia climbs in. The animals have disappeared under the foam, but Olivia picks them out one by one, singing a verse from Old Macdonald's Farm about each one. She scrubs each animal with a nailbrush and makes it do a crazy dance on the side of the bath, before dropping it onto the floor. She makes me laugh.

When all the animals are clean, Olivia looks at me and says, "Do you miss Green?"

I nod. "Kind of."

"Mo saved his life. She's a super hero."

"Yeah," I say. "Mo's a super hero."

"Cool," says Olivia.

She starts splashing me with bubbles and I splash her back. We laugh a lot, and it's nice. Olivia is the closest thing I have to a sister and I'll miss her when I'm gone, but somewhere out there I have a brother.

"What are you thinking?" she says, suddenly, looking me straight in the eyes.

I shrug. "Nothing. Why? What are you thinking?"

And she says, "I love Mo too."

"Too?"

She nods. "I love Sid, and I love Green, and I love Mo too."

"That's nice," I say. "You should tell her."

She's still looking at me. And then she says. "And I love you."

I don't expect it. And I don't know what to say back.

Are those three short words game changers? Because suddenly I regret everything. Maybe family isn't just about flesh and blood after all. I don't want to *never* see this family again, but I don't want *never* to see Mum again either.

I don't know what to do.

While Olivia gets herself dressed, I sit on the stairs and play with confessions in my head. If only I could find the words to say what I need to say and not get anyone in trouble. Or maybe I could ring Mum and tell her it's off; tell her I don't want to go to Australia? I could get the money back and no one would be any the wiser … except she'd still be wanted and I might not see her again for another six years ... or worse. And I might still have to go to HOME from HOME. If only there was a way to start over again and do it differently...

The telephone rings and I'm nearest, so I answer.

It's the garage to say the van is ready for collection.

"Who was that?" says Mo, coming out of the kitchen.

"Erm … the garage?" I say without thinking.

"Is the van ready?"

I should have said wrong number. If Sid collects it today, he'll discover the money is missing. "Erm ... it's going to be another day or two … maybe three. They'll ring when it's done," I say.

Mo pulls a face. "That's not good. It must be a bigger job that we all thought."

I think I've bought myself some time, but when she breaks the news to Sid, he hits the roof.

"Not ready? NOT READY?" he shouts. "What do they think they're playing at?" He grabs the phone and punches in a number. "You can't just leave a family dangling, waiting for their wheels ... Oh hello? Yes, this is Sidney Love. What's going on? You promised my van would be ready... What? ... It is? ... But someone phoned to say it wasn't ..."

I move towards the door while thinking up a second lie to cover my first.

"...Thank you. Yes, I'll be along shortly. Thank you."

"So it is ready?" says Mo.

"Yes, a misunderstanding. We can collect today."

And Sid is so made up about the van being actually ready he doesn't quiz me about the so-called misunderstanding. I think I've gotten away with it until he heads to the bureau.

My blood curdles and I feel sick inside.

"It's not here!" he shouts.

Mo goes through to the living room. Olivia comes running downstairs and joins them. I hang around in the doorway, trying to look invisible. Sid shuffles pieces of paper about in case the money is buried underneath one of them.

"Did you move it?" he says to Mo, panicking.

"Definitely not."

"But it's not here," says Sid.

"Oh don't be silly. It's there. Of course it's there." She joins him at the bureau and together they start sifting through every single scrap of paper and file in front of them.

I'm just about to leave when they both turn and look at me. Their eyes burn into my soul. I'm a thief. From a long line of thieves. First Mum, now me.

"What?" I say, trying to pretend I don't know they know.

And then Mo says, "Elle, have you moved the van money?"

"Why would I move it?"

Mo wrinkles her nose, as if she doesn't believe me, but even so she still doesn't actually come out and accuse me of theft.

Sid does though. "You've taken it, Elle, haven't you?"

"What would I do with £500?" I say.

And then Sid says, "Did you also lie about the van not being ready?"

I chew the inside of my cheek. There's no way out of this, but still I say, "No!"

Mo and Sid look at each other. I don't know what they're going to do next.

Olivia hides behind Sid, as if I'm some kind of monster. I protest my innocence again.

Mo steps forward, calmly, and takes my hand. She says, "We will fight to keep you here, Elle. We love you and we want you to stay. But you *have* to tell us the truth."

She doesn't deserve me, the liar and the thief, and the cheater. Even when she knows all this about me, she still says she wants me here. I should confess ... but I can't. I can't live with the shame, and anyway, my own mum, my real mum, came back for me... kind of...

"I didn't take the money," I say. Mo lets go of my hand and steps away.

Sid says, "Then we need to call the police."

"No!" I say, too forcefully. "You can't!"

He shrugs. "We've had a thief in our house and we need to report it to the police."

I'm lost.

Dead.

I can't win.

And my heart is thumping so hard I think it's going to topple me over. So I run, out of the room, up to my bedroom where I fall on the bed and pull the duvet over my head praying for a miracle.

29.

It's Olivia who gives me away.

"Elle's going out!" she shouts.

I open the door, ready to run, but Sid is lightning and leaps in front of me before I am free. "Not so fast. We need to sit down and talk about this."

I fold my arms and look him square in the eye. "I don't have anything to say."

His body doesn't move, but one slightly raised eyebrow stops me pushing past him.

Mo joins us at the door. "Please Elle? Just come and sit with us for a while."

I shake my head. "No," I say. "I need some fresh air. I need to think this through." Is that an admission of guilt? I don't care if it is. I'm not sitting down, or talking, or listening.

Sid and Mo look at each other. I wonder if they've already called the police. But no, they wouldn't be trying to '*talk about this*' if they had. Mo tips her head slightly to one side and smiles, like she's trying to understand. It's not the kind of confrontation I'm used to. This would be so much easier if they shouted or ordered me to my room; but I don't know how to fight cocked eyebrows and lopsided smiles. I need new a tactic.

"Please? I won't go far," I lie. "Just give me some thinking space."

You can see Mo weighing it up, thinking about it. Sid's sticking with the eyebrow.

"Okay," says Mo, after a while. "Take a few minutes. But don't go far. And take this..." She hands me her mobile phone. "Call us when you're ready to come home. We'll have tea and some biscuits and try to find a way forward. Yes?"

They are too nice, and I don't deserve it.

I'm a horrible person. I've stolen money from them and still they trust me with Mo's mobile phone ... but my mum – MY REAL MUM – might be waiting for me to start a new life in Australia and live happily ever after. But even if she isn't, even if Billy Slade has done a bunk with the money, even if Mum doesn't really want me ... I can't stay here.

"I don't need your phone," I say. "I've got my own."

Mo nods. "Don't be too long, eh?"

"Okay," I say. But I have no intention of going back.

I walk down the road, looking at all the other perfect houses with their perfect lawns and their perfectly shiny new cars, and then I look back at the Love house, with its peeling paint, and pothole garden. It's been easy living here. Comfortable. For the first time ever, I felt heard. I felt as if I was a good me, not the bad, useless, always-in-the-way me. And I do feel sad to be leaving. I wonder if this is how Mum felt when she walked out on me in the bank. Her choice wasn't that much different to mine; stay with the family you love, or walk away to a better life ... Did she love me, though?

Do I love Mo and Sid? Olivia? And Green?

Strangely, when I think of Green my eyes prickle and I want to cry. Cactus prickles. I laugh, then laugh and cry at the same time. And by the time I reach the end of the road, tears are flowing freely down my cheeks because I don't know what I'm doing with my life.

I don't even know what I'm doing now.

I am a wretched useless failure. A thief. A liar.

"Are you all right, Ducky?" says an old lady on a mobility scooter. I've never met her before and she doesn't know anything about me, but she seems to care.

"Fuck off!" I say.

She's shocked. I'm shocked. Why did I say that?

Because the real me, *IS* bad and useless and ruins everything good.

When I'm out of sight of the house, I dial Mum's number.

A man answers. Billy Slade. "What?" he says.

"It's Elle."

"And?"

"Is Mum there?"

I hear him shout Mum's name, and then the phone goes all crackly and although I can hear talking, it's muffled and I can't understand the words.

"Hello? ... Hello?" I say. "Is that you, Mum?"

There's no reply. The line goes dead. It must be a bad signal. So I try again.

The phone rings. It rings and rings but no one answers, and eventually goes to voicemail. I don't bother to leave a message. Maybe the battery went dead? In which case, Mum will be looking for a charger. I sit on a wall and give her a minute or two before I try again.

A lone magpie lands in the road before me and hops around pecking at the gravel. There's nothing there to eat. She must be desperate. I feel for her.

I try Mum's number again. It goes straight to voicemail so I hang up and try again.

Same thing.

One more time. She must have found her charger by now?

But the seed of doubt – the seed I have so far refused to cultivate – is growing, bursting into life with shoots and leaves and prickles even Green would be proud of.

I can ignore it no longer.

Mum is never going to answer her phone. This is like last time, when she took the money and never came back. This is third time unlucky. Because three times now she's chosen money over me – her daughter. Once in the bank, once outside school, and now ... when not only has she taken my money – Sid's money – she's condemned me to a life in HOME from HOME.

I fight back the thoughts now trying to strangle me. I try to convince myself of things I know in my heart to be lies.

I haven't been betrayed.
I haven't been dumped.
I haven't been used.
BECAUSE MUM WOULDN'T DO THAT TO ME.
And when my phone rings, my heart rallies...
But the caller ID says, MO.
I answer. I've nothing left to lose.

30.

"Elle? Where are you?" says Mo. "I need to go to the hospital ... come home, now."

There's an urgency in her voice I don't even question. I just turn around and start running back towards the house. By the time I get there, a taxi is outside. Mo is about to get in.

"Thank goodness you're here," she says. "I have to go and see Dad. But I need to know you're home and safe while I'm gone. Will you stay here, with Sid and Olivia? Please?"

I look at Olivia snuggled into Sid's arms. And I look back at Mo, alone, tears in her eyes. "Can I come with you?" I say, feeling her pain. "Keep you company?"

Mo doesn't answer, just looks from me to Sid and back again.

"I won't be any trouble. Promise."

So Mo nods, and I climb into the taxi next to her.

And then Olivia says, "I want to come too!"

"No, Olivia, we'll stay here," says Sid. "Play a game."

"I don't want to play a game. I want to see Green."

Sid looks at Mo. "What do you think?"

Mo sighs. "Come on then ... let's all go."

Olivia squeezes in between Mo and I and Sid gets into the front. We buckle up and the taxi speeds off towards the hospital. I wonder out loud what has happened to Green.

Mo looks out the window. "Dad's had another fall," she says, her voice wobbling, trying to hold back the emotion.

"Is he going to die?" wonders Olivia, starting to cry.

Mo shakes her head, but I get the feeling it's not an answer to the question; it's because she doesn't want to answer it. And that makes me want to cry again. I don't know if it's for me, or Green, or why.

The taxi pulls into the 'emergency vehicles only' space and we all pile out. Mo bundles us through a couple of big red doors into a reception area, while Sid haggles with the taxi driver about the fare.

Inside the hospital, Mo says, "Wait with Olivia while I find out what's what."

She puts Olivia's hand in mine and wraps my other hand around it. Glue. Olivia doesn't wriggle or try to escape. She doesn't need glue. Her face is white and she's unnervingly quiet.

I hear myself say, "It's okay, Olivia. Everything will be all right." But what do I know?

Mo speaks to a lady sitting behind a glass partition. Olivia and I sit on the two free chairs in an otherwise crowded waiting room. A TV in the corner is broadcasting a football match. On the walls are pictures of mountains, the sea and the countryside, as well as a large notice about treating staff with respect and a warning that bad behaviour will not be tolerated. The people around us are either talking in whispers or saying nothing. Some of them have obvious injuries, cuts or bandages, but others have nothing visible. There's a funny smell, of disinfectant, and coffee. I hate it here. It's gloomy and sad. Olivia moves off her chair and sits on my knee.

Mo comes back to join us. "Dad's in the oncology unit, on the fifth floor," she says. "We can wait up there."

We find a lift.

Mo lets Olivia press the buttons and tells her to count the floors as we go up and up. "But make sure we don't go too high and fly into the sky!" She's trying to make light of it, to reassure Olivia – and maybe herself – but her heart is not in it and Olivia doesn't bother counting.

I whisper to Mo. "Isn't oncology something to do with cancer?"

Mo nods but doesn't elaborate.

At the fifth floor, there's another waiting room, with less people, more windows, and the same disinfectant smell. Mo checks in at a reception desk.

"The doctors are with Dad at the moment," she says when she re-joins us. Her voice is shaky. "They'll let us know when we can go see him." She looks anxiously between her watch and the lift door, mumbling something about Sid taking his time.

I offer to go and find him, but Mo shakes her head, says he'll work it out. So I pick a magazine from a pile on a table – Hollywood Gossip. There's a picture of Zac on the front. I find a comic for Olivia. We both flick through the pages, not really reading; just passing time. Hollywood gossip isn't enough to take my mind off now.

When Sid eventually appears, he explains the delay. He didn't have enough cash for the taxi fair and after pleading with the taxi driver, had to leave his watch as payment. I feel really bad about that. It's my fault he doesn't have enough cash and my fault he doesn't have a van which could have driven us here. But neither Sid nor Mo looks at me with blame or recrimination in their eyes. I guess they have bigger things on their minds right now.

When Olivia starts to get fidgety, Mo suggests a game to pass the time.

"I-spy?" says Sid.

"I hate I-spy," says Olivia.

Sid picks a magazine from the table, and says, "So how about we choose one of the pictures in this magazine, and then we take it in turns to make up a story about it."

Olivia doesn't want to do that either.

And neither do I.

But Mo is encouraging and puts on a brave face. "Come on," she says. "It'll be fun. I'll go first." She flicks through the pages – the pictures aren't especially inspiring – but she stops at a picture of a woman lying on a beach in her swimming costume. "Once upon a time," she says, "there was a beautiful woman who liked to lie on the beach and sunbathe. On this particular day, it was very very hot, and after a while, she fell asleep. While she was asleep, a robber came and stole her purse and her sandwiches and all her clothes! And when she woke up, she had nothing except her swimming costume!"

Olivia giggles.

"So what do you think she did?"

"Phoned Batman?" says Olivia.

"Excellent," says Mo. "Now you tell us the next bit of the story."

Olivia scratches her head and I'm thinking she'll never come up with anything, but then from the deeper recesses of her tiny Batman obsessed brain, she does. "Well, Batman and Robin came straight away. Batman told Robin to give the lady his cloak, but Robin said it would make him cold, and Batman told him not to be selfish and give it to the lady who was even colder. And then they went shopping in the Batmobile and bought the lady some more sandwiches."

"What flavour?" says Sid.

"Erm ... strawberry and banana," says Olivia. "But you interrupted me so now it's your turn."

"Fair enough," says Sid. He thinks for a minute, and then in a really funny California sissy girl kind of voice, says, "Oh Batman, these are delicious. How did you know they were my favourite flavour?"

Olivia and I both giggle.

And then in a deep, manly voice, Sid says, "I'm Batman. I know everything. I know who stole your sandwiches ..." he looks at me when he says that "...and I also know that he had a good reason." Switch to high voice. "What, Batman? Tell me, what would drive a person to steal someone's last crust of bread?" Low voice. "Need, Madam, not greed. And we have to help that poor robber so that he – or *she* – need never be hungry again."

Olivia chips in then. "Aren't you going to biff him or squish him or send him to jail?"

Low voice. "Not this time, Madam. This time, I'm going to show mercy..."

A woman comes over to us and asks to speak to Mo.

Mo goes with her, out of earshot.

Olivia says, "This is a rubbish story."

Again, Sid looks me squarely in the eye, and in his own voice says, "Sometimes it's better to listen and understand, than judge and punish."

I know he's talking to me. I know he wants me to tell him about the money. But I can't. Not here. Not in front of Olivia. So I say, "Is it my turn?"

Sid nods.

Olivia says, "Come on, Elle. Do a proper Batman story."

So I say, "Yeah, so after the lady had eaten her sandwiches, Batman and Robin drove her home. The woman was really grateful and went and put some clothes on, so Robin got his cape back, and then she said sorry for being such a lot of trouble and if Batman could please go and biff the robber for being so stupid, she would totally understand."

"No no no," says Sid. "No biffing allowed in this story."

"Who says?" says Olivia.

"Erm... I DO!" says Sid, in a big booming voice. "BECAUSE I AM SUPERBATMAN, FATHER OF ALL THE BAT MEN AND THE BAT ROBINS..."

It's silly. We giggle, and only stop when Mo comes back.

"Dad's ready," she says. "We can go and visit him now."

"Hooray," says Olivia, jumping up from the floor.

Sid frowns and looks at Mo questioningly. She shakes her head. Of course, she wasn't with the nurse all that time just to hear Green is fine. Which means he's not. It means there's a problem – cancer – she doesn't want to tell us about. Because we're kids. A couple of kids, no relation. And one of us is a thief and probably won't be staying very long anyway...

"Come along now," says Mo. "Let's go and cheer Dad up." She smiles with her mouth but her eyes are still sad.

31.

Green's in a little room on his own. His head is drooping and his eyes are closed. His skin is grey. He's hooked up to all sorts of electronic machinery with buttons and lights all flashing and bleeping away, and a drip of clear fluid feeds into his arm.

Mo touches his hand. His head lifts; he smiles when he sees us and his skin seems to regain a little of its colour.

"The family!" he says, weakly. "Maureen and Sidney. And the girls. How lovely to see you." His voice is thin, as if it's not really Green speaking.

Olivia climbs onto the bed. Sid swiftly picks her up and puts her back on the floor. She complains because she wants to cuddle Green and make him feel better.

"Yes, but Maurice isn't really up to it at the moment," says Sid. "How about holding his hand?"

Olivia's bottom lip sticks out and she folds her arms defiantly.

"I know what *would* make me feel better," says Green feebly.

"What?"

"Well I haven't had my newspaper today and I *think* there might be money in my pocket…"

Green looks around, then points to a small cupboard. Sid opens the door, pulls out Green's clothes, and there is indeed, a five pound note in his trouser pocket.

"Would you and Sid like to buy a Gazette for me? And if they've got any comics … "

Olivia takes the money and remembers to say thank you.

"And find something nice for Elle too," says Green. He smiles at me.

Sid takes Olivia's hand, tells her to walk nicely, and they leave.

Mo and I pull up two chairs close to the bed.

"How are you feeling?" says Mo.

"Dreadful," says Green. "I'd be better if they took these wires away."

"Give it time," says Mo, "and you'll be right as rain."

"Let's not fool ourselves, Maureen," he says.

Mo flashes him a look of disapproval.

He shrugs.

We don't say anything for a while and my eyes wander around the room at all the gadgets and gismos. He looks tired and beaten. Mo looks upset. I don't know how I feel. I'm totally numb.

"Are you in pain?" says Mo, eventually.

"Not anymore," says Green. He points at the drip going into his arm. "This helps."

Mo nods. "Sorry," she says.

Green shakes his head, dismissively.

It's quiet again.

There's nothing to do but think, and remember, and wonder why this is upsetting me so much. It's not as if Green is any relation. I didn't even like him when we first met. But something changed. And now I'm sad he's here and looking so ill and I want everything to go back to normal – whatever that is – except it won't.

Not ever.

And that's got nothing to do with Green.

Mo breaks the ice again. She starts talking about baking and how Miriam has asked if she can do some lemon drizzle cake slices. Apparently, Green likes lemon drizzle cake. "I'll bring you some in," says Mo.

"Thank you, Maureen. I'd like that," says Green.

"And we'll have a party when you come home," she says. "Won't we Elle?"

I nod, wondering if I'll be there when Green comes home.

We don't speak again. I listen to the noises outside Green's little room – trolleys, people talking, telephones – and the beeping of the machines keeping tabs on Green. It's hard to know what to say.

And then Green asks me, "Are you all prepared for that audition thing at the college?"

I look at Mo. She looks away, doesn't speak.

"I don't think I'll be doing it," I say. "Not now."

"Why not?" says Green,

I laugh, an embarrassed kind of laugh. "It's complicated."

Green shrugs. "Life's complicated. You should still give it a go. What have you got to lose?"

I don't answer. Olivia bursts in, waving a Gazette, a Wonder Woman comic and a bag of jelly sweets for me, but she's alone.

"Where's Sid?" I say.

"We had a race," says Olivia. "I won."

So we wait, expecting Sid to appear, and while we wait, Green puts on a smiley face. He leaves the newspaper untouched, but he and Olivia look at the comic together and Green makes a big deal out of Olivia being the next Wonder Woman. I'm not hungry for jelly sweets.

"I'd better go and find Sid," says Mo when he still doesn't arrive. She grabs Olivia's hand, and tells me to wait here. "You'll be all right for a minute?" she says, a statement which comes out like a question.

I nod. She leaves. It's just Green and me.

And I'm *not* all right. I wrack my brain for something to talk about but I don't know what to say, so I stand up and peer out of the window, fold Green's trousers and put them back in his locker. He doesn't speak either, just watches my avoidance activity.

Eventually I pluck up the courage to ask him what's wrong.

"I've got a tumour, Elle, in my brain. I've known about it for a while, but I didn't want anyone to worry."

"Mo knew something was wrong," I said. "So she worried anyway."

He laughs. "She knows the truth now."

I don't know what to say. And I can't help feeling that Mo should be with her dad and that I should have been the one to go and find Sid. Just another thing to feel guilty about. I stand up and open the door. There's no sign of Mo or Sid or Olivia anywhere.

And then Green says, "Is everything okay, Elle?"

"Why wouldn't it be?"

"Because I may be old and on my way out, but I can tell something's wrong."

"I don't want to talk about it," I say, and change the subject, "When are you coming home, anyway?"

And Green says, "An alien life form has taken control of my body. I don't think I will be coming home, however much Maureen wills it."

I catch my breath.

"But I've had a good innings," he says. "And I've put everything right ... thanks to you."

"Me?"

"You and the Purple Emperor. I couldn't have done that without you."

"That's not true" I say. "You were going to do it before I threw your stinking rubbish away."

"That's what I wanted you to think ... but in real life? I'd probably never have gone through with it. You made the difference, Elle. You. You were the difference between failure and success. And seeing that damned butterfly brought me closer to Alice than I've been in years. I'm grateful for what you gave me."

One minute I'm the worst person in the world, beyond help, beyond hope. And the next, I'm the difference between failure and success. Redeemable? And it's funny that Green, of all people, should be the one to make me feel like that.

"So come on," he says. "Tell me what's bothering you."

Where would I even start? The lies? The stealing? The van? Or Mum and Billy Slade?

"Elle," he says, gently. "It's important to put things right in your life whenever you get the chance."

"What if it's too late?"

"It's never too late."

I suck my lips in and think about what everyone would say if I told them the truth. And then I remember Sid's story. They already know I stole the money and lied. They just don't know why.

"Find a way to be happy, Elle. Laugh, sing, star in one of your movies. Do whatever it takes, because life is short and happiness is the only thing that matters."

"But how can I be happy when my own mum doesn't want me?" Saying it out loud stabs my heart and puts me on the edge of tears again.

"I've seen you laughing, and smiling," he says. "I've seen plenty of happy moments."

"But I want my Mum, my own Mum and my own family. Why can't I have that?"

Green holds up his hand for me to stop. "If you spend your whole life chasing a butterfly you'll forget to notice the flowers."

"Are you calling my mum a butterfly?" I say.

"I've never met your mum, but yes, I've a feeling she might be, because butterflies aren't meant to be caught. Butterflies are programmed to fly away." He closes his eyes. He's tired. "Especially those pesky Purple Emperors."

I think about his words. Even if I did manage to catch Mum and hold her in one place, I'd always be thinking about her next flight, so maybe Green is right. Maybe Mo is right. Maybe it's time to let go?

Mo, Sid and Olivia return, followed by a nurse. She checks the electronics and says Green's had enough for one day and we should leave. Mo would like some time alone with her dad, but Sid, Olivia and I say our goodbyes and promise to come back soon. Sid shakes hands with Green and tells him we'll be back soon. Olivia thanks him for the comic. I hug Green and whisper, "Thank you, for everything," into his ear. I'm not sure he hears.

And then we go.

*

When the house phone rings in the middle of the night, I know it is bad news.

It's never too late to put things right, Green said.

Find a way to be happy, he said.

Laugh, sing, star in movie.

Remember to look at the flowers.

I made a difference to Green's life, and if that good feeling isn't going to die with him, I have to make a difference in my own.

32.

Breakfast is grim. There's a Green shaped hole at the table and no one feels like talking or eating. Afterwards, Mo has phone calls and arrangements to make. Sid does his best to occupy Olivia with some homemade play dough. He asks me to join in but I need to be alone. It's time to do the right thing.

I go up to my room and dial the police non-emergency number. I tell them I know where Stevie Mackenzie, wanted for armed robbery, might be. I give them my address and crucially I am able to tell them the number plate of Mum's bike – QZR 123.

And then I dial Sasha's number…

Sasha is at the house within minutes. I watch for her car coming up the road, and let her in before she needs to knock. When I show her through to the living room, Mo and Sid are surprised.

"Oh!" says Mo. "I'm sorry, but it's not a good time..."

Sasha looks at me.

I swallow. I can't back out now. This is my chance to prove I'm more than a liar and a thief; to end the living nightmare of my own personal groundhog day and put things right with the only family who have ever really cared about me. "I asked her to come," I say. "And I know my timing is lousy, but I've got something to tell you all."

And that's what I do. I tell these adults – and Olivia too – everything. About Mum, the money, the van. About Australia and Billy Slade and motorbikes ... I tell them about the letters, the hope, the disappointment, the number of the Harley that drove away with Sid's money – the money he was saving to go to see his own mum. And I tell them I think I might have a brother. I hope the police catch Mum before she's too far away, because I want her to face up to her past, in the way that I am now. I want people to know the truth.

I don't want to be that girl – the girl whose mother robbed a bank – anymore.

And then I stand in front of Sid, and say, "I'm truly sorry. I took your chance to see your mum away, so that I could be with mine. And I am, really sorry..." As the words tumble from my mouth, a weight is lifted from me. I feel lighter somehow. Easier. Having nothing to hide makes everything less complicated and the future – wherever it is – doesn't frighten me anymore. "And I'll get a job. I'll pay you back. I promise."

"It's okay, Elle," says Sid, generously. "I understand. I'll go see Mum next year."

Mo comes over and wraps her arms around me. "Everything is going to be all right," she says. "You've done the right thing and I'm so so proud of you for that." There's a crack in her voice and tears in her eyes. I'm not sure if they are for me, or Green.

"If I have to go to HOME from HOME, I won't fight it," I say.

"We have never wanted you go to there, Elle. You must know that," says Mo.

I pull away, and look at Sasha.

She shuffles pieces of paper in a folder and doesn't speak for ages. I'm hoping and praying all the time she is silent, that a miracle will occur.

"Well?" says Mo.

"Obviously I can't make any decisions here and now, but it's good that you've told the truth at last, Elle. We'll see what we can do..."

"And what about this brother?" says Mo. "Is there any way we can trace him?"

Sasha nods. "Again, we'll see what we can do."

There isn't time to say anything else. A policeman and a policewoman have arrived and need to take a statement. It's the same man who Green tried to give his little book of numbers to. He wouldn't take that, but he's very interested in QZR 123.

33.

I've never been to a funeral before, but it isn't what I expect. The crematorium is packed. For someone who kept himself to himself for so long, there are an awful lot of people wanting to say goodbye.

"It's a celebration of Dad's life, more than anything," says Mo.

There's no religious ceremony because Green didn't believe in God or life after death but there is a very nice woman called Kath, the celebrant, who does a lot of talking about Green's life. Several of his police friends also stand up and talk about some of Green's more famous moments as a police officer.

There is a lot of love for him and that surprises me, not because I didn't also come to love him at the end, but because the Green I knew was spiky and cranky and difficult to live with ... but maybe I only saw him after the alien had taken up residence in his body?

Afterwards, we all go to the community centre where there are cakes – dozens of cakes – including one in the shape of a Purple Emperor butterfly.

Mo and Sid share stories about family times, and then Olivia stands up and says he was a super hero. Mo asks me if I want to say anything and I do. I go to the front and stand there, looking at all the people Green has known, who cared about him. I try to speak, and fail. If I could get the words out, I would tell everyone what Green taught me: that it's never too late to put things right, to find a way to be happy, and of course, to look at the flowers.

After

It's audition day, and I still can't believe I'm actually going for it. I stand in front of my bedroom mirror and recite my poem, over and over, so I don't forget the words. And when I'm happy with it, I do some vocal warm-ups Sid taught me; some humming, some tongue twisters; "Unique New York, Unique New York, Unique New York ... A big black bug bit a big black bear ... How much wood could a woodchuck chuck if a woodchuck could chuck wood?" and then the tonic sol-fa scale, "Do Re Mi Fa Sol La Ti Do."

As I'm singing the scale, I notice Olivia standing in my doorway. She is cuddling her spider and holding her new lunch box, ready for her first day at school. She looks terrified.

"You okay, Olivia?"

She nods, but she doesn't look okay.

"Are you worrying about school?"

She nods again.

I open my arms and she comes over to me for a reassuring hug. I stroke her hair. "You'll be fine," I tell her. "Everyone will love you, and you'll have a great day."

"I'm scared," she says.

"I know," I say. "I'm scared too. But think how brave we are? Doing something when you're scared is real bravery."

"Yes," says Olivia. "I like being brave. And I am, really brave. Like Batman's brave. Yeah, I'm brave, aren't I? Really really brave. "

I laugh. It's so simple when you're five.

"And Sid's brave too."

"Of course he is," I say. "And Mo."

"We're the brave family," says Olivia. "That means I'm really lucky."

"Yeah, we're lucky too," I say.

"Because we've got Mo and Sid who love us, and we've got each other, and we've got this nice house, and a garden... and Lego."

"Yes, and Lego, and toys..."

"And cakes. We've got lots of cakes."

I laugh again. "Yeah. And we've got the best cakes in the world."

"And we can play super heroes after school, can't we?"

"Yeah!" I say. "I can't wait."

Downstairs, the table is set for a party; a breakfast party! There are toasted sandwiches and crisps and cakes of all shapes and sizes. The centrepiece is a birthday cake in the shape of Batwoman.

"That was my idea!" says Olivia.

"But when did you do all this?" I can't believe they did it without me knowing.

"Mo and Sid did it while you were asleep!" says Olivia.

I feel my eyes prickle with tears. "I love it," I say. "Thank you."

Mo and Sid and Olivia treat me like a princess. There is a little present and a card to open. The present is a small oval locket. It has a picture of Mo and Sid and Olivia inside. The card is a drawing of Batman and Batwoman, done by Olivia, and it's so sweet.

"I don't deserve this," I say. "But thank you."

Over breakfast, Mo tells me that Sasha has started to make some enquiries about my brother, and as soon as they know anything they'll be in touch. Zayna texts me and we arrange to meet after the audition, with Tess and Sophie. And we talk about all the things Olivia and I have to look forward to. It's possibly the happiest I have ever been in my life.

I am brushing my teeth when I hear the phone ring.

Mo answers, but calls Sid immediately. She sounds excited.

I rush to the landing to listen.

"Yes? Yes? YES!" says Sid to the caller. He puts the phone down and shouts, "YES!" one more time, fist punching the air.

I run down the stairs. "What is it?" we all want to know.

"Remember the audition … the one I didn't get to because of the van?" He doesn't wait for an answer. "Well, the other guy, the one they offered the part to ... he can't do it. They want me to be Superdad!"

Olivia, throws her arms around Sid.

And then we fall into each other's arms – a tangle of hope and excitement and I wish Green was here to share this moment, but in many ways, he is.

- End -

Also by Wendy Storer

BRING ME SUNSHINE
WINNER of the Children's & Young Adult category of the 2018 International Rubery Book Award
FINALIST in the Mslexia Children's Novel Competition 2013
Bring Me Sunshine is an inspirational story about following your heart, never giving up and living in the moment.

WHERE BLUEBIRDS FLY
Where Bluebirds Fly is a moving story about making friends with your enemy, dumping your past and daring to hope.

Coming Soon…
BORN LUCKY

For more information about Wendy Storer,
please visit her website
www.wendystorer.ws

Printed in Great Britain
by Amazon